TARA-LEIGH COBBLE

HE'S WHERE THE JOY IS

GETTING TO KNOW THE CAPTIVATING
GOD OF THE TRINITY

Lifeway Press®
Nashville, TN

EDITORIAL TEAM,
LIFEWAY WOMEN
PUBLISHING

Becky Loyd
Director, Lifeway Women

Tina Boesch
Manager, Lifeway Women
Publishing

Sarah Doss
Editorial Project Leader,
Lifeway Women Publishing

Mike Wakefield
Content Editor

Erin Franklin
Production Editor

Chelsea Waack
Graphic Designer

Lauren Ervin
Cover Designer

Published by Lifeway Press® · © 2021 Tara-Leigh Cobble

ISBN: 978-1-0877-3984-7

Item: 005831206

Dewey decimal classification: 231.044

Subject heading: GOD / JESUS CHRIST—DIVINITY / TRINITY / HOLY SPIRIT

To order additional copies of this resource, write Lifeway Resources Customer Service; One Lifeway Plaza; Nashville, TN 37234; FAX order to 615.251.5933; call toll-free 800.458.2772; email orderentry@lifeway.com; or order online at lifeway.com.

Printed in the United States of America

Lifeway Women Publishing,
Lifeway Resources,
One Lifeway Plaza,
Nashville, TN 37234

TABLE OF CONTENTS

ABOUT THE AUTHOR

Tara-Leigh Cobble's zeal for biblical literacy led her to create D-Group (Discipleship Group), which has grown into an international network of three hundred-plus Bible studies that meet every week in homes, churches, and online. She also writes and hosts a daily radio show called *The God Shot*, as well as a daily podcast called *The Bible Recap* which unpacks the richness of Scripture alongside the chronological one-year reading plan. In just over two years, the podcast garnered seventy million downloads and reached number three on the Apple Podcast top overall charts. More than twenty thousand churches around the world have joined their reading plan to know and love God better. Her book, *The Bible Recap*, a 365-day guide to reading through the Bible, aims to help people not only read and understand Scripture but *love* it too!

A WORD FROM THE AUTHOR

If you had to describe God's personality, what would you say? Not what He does, but His demeanor. Not what He's capable of, but what He's like.

Here's how King David described God: "in your presence there is fullness of joy; at your right hand are pleasures forevermore" (Ps. 16:11). He also said God's presence brings gladness and joy (Ps. 21:6)!

Does it surprise you to know that God is happy? He is infinitely joyful! And because He's so delighted, that's how He can be delightful to us—by sharing who He is with us. If joy is your goal, knowing the triune God will be supremely useful to you. In fact, this is the only path to true joy.

But that doesn't mean it will be an easy path. Everything beautiful in life has some level of unavoidable difficulty attached to it, including our best and strongest relationships. In every relationship, you have to go through the process of getting to know the other person. Along the way you face misunderstandings and miscommunications; maybe you also encounter unmet expectations—all as a part of building the relationship. People are wonderfully complex, aren't we?

Our relationship with God has a lot of those same complexities because He's a Person too. Three Persons, actually—Father, Son, and Spirit. You're likely here because you already agree with the idea of the trinitarian God of the Bible, but you don't necessarily know what that means. So, to a certain degree, I'll assume we're on the same page and that I don't need to spend paragraphs or pages convincing you God exists or the Bible is true. However, even those of us who consent to belief in the Trinity have a hard time grasping exactly what (or Who?) it is (They are?). See how complex it already feels?

J. I. Packer said the doctrine of the Trinity "confronts us with perhaps the most difficult thought that the human mind has ever been asked to handle. It is not easy; but it is true."[1] Someone once said, "If you don't believe in the Trinity, you will lose your soul. But if you try to understand it, you will lose your mind."[2] It's true that some things are beyond our complete knowledge, but they aren't beyond our partial knowledge. So in this study, we'll make it our aim to know the highest percentage of what our minds can possibly grasp. After all, knowing Him is the path to joy, and I want as much joy as possible.

What makes this doctrine so challenging? Why do people tend to brush over it instead of dig in? Here are a few things that contribute to our collective confusion and difficulty with the Trinity.

Simplified explanations

If you've ever been part of a Bible study or a Sunday School class that talked about the Trinity, you've likely heard analogies of shamrocks and eggs and H_2O. Maybe someone has drawn a picture of a triangle or a shield. Every analogy of the Trinity breaks down at some level, simply because there's nothing else in existence quite like God. Everything else has a point of origin and relies on the things around it for its definition, but God is uncreated and has always been who He is.

Some analogies are better than others, but even those require caveats. Other analogies are downright heretical—which is to say, they tell more of a lie about God than a truth, and they're more harmful than helpful in giving us a right view of God. (See a list of heresies on p. 215.) He isn't dependent on anything else to be who He is, so when we compare Him to something that inherently is dependent on something else, it will always lead us down the wrong path. We crave analogies because they seem to help simplify God, and we prefer to simplify Him because it's easier than studying His complexity. But is that how you want to be known? Is that how you aim to build a relationship with anyone you love? Simplified explanations fall short of being enlightening or fulfilling in our relationship with God.

Selfishness

This answer may not apply to you, but it certainly does to me. My selfishness was one of the biggest hurdles that kept me from digging into the Trinity. I preferred to focus on God's promises to me and all the things He could do to benefit me, so I was content to stop short of looking for who He is. I tuned out when someone mentioned the Trinity—not because I already knew all the details, but because I didn't yet know enough. I was in for a real surprise when I did begin to study the Trinity. It isn't just a theological concept; fundamentally, it's a relationship. To have a healthy, functioning relationship, you have to look beyond yourself and get to know the other person involved.

The Bible never uses the word *Trinity*.

However, that doesn't mean the triune God is not addressed in Scripture. In fact, we'll read more Trinity-related passages in this study than you can imagine! The idea of the Trinity is found throughout the Bible, starting in Genesis 1:1. Jesus talked about it in the Gospels, and the apostles affirmed it throughout their New Testament letters. Still, the early church struggled to summarize it until a theologian named Tertullian, who lived about a century after Jesus' resurrection, created the word *Trinity* to succinctly reference Scripture's teaching about God.[3]

(By the way, many books cover how and why and when the early church named and articulated the doctrine of the Trinity as it appears in Scripture. Other books investigate the original words and languages used in Scripture to explain the Trinity. And there are still others that show how the Trinity is unique to Christianity and how our triune God stands in stark contrast to the gods of other religions. We won't cover those topics in-depth, but in case you're interested in learning more about any of them, I've built out a list of suggestions on p. 219.)

This doctrine is absolutely necessary to the Christian faith. Its importance can't be overemphasized. Theologian Ligon Duncan said that asking, *Is the identity of the Trinity important to the Gospel?* is similar to asking, "Is who your wife is central to your marriage?"[4] Without the Trinity as the core of our beliefs, every other doctrine of our faith starts to come unglued and unhinged. You cannot have the Christian faith without a triune God. This is a bold statement, but the creeds support it. (See pp. 216–218 to read the Athanasian Creed.) Every other Christian belief is built on this foundation. Without it, we slide into the cultic beliefs of Mormons, Jehovah's Witnesses, or Muslims.

It's tempting to diminish the importance of the Trinity and to seek a false peace by simply "focusing on the Word of God." But that's shallow at best and foolish at least. In fact, God's Word is precisely where we learn about His Persons; He's given it to us so we can know Him in greater depth. How heartless and arrogant to want to know less of Him than He has made possible. People who truly know God have always wanted to know God more—both for their own sakes and for the sake of being able to talk more clearly about Him and His love with others. So I'm glad you're here, trying—digging in. And I know God smiles at it too. He loves to be known and understood and loved, just like you love to be known and understood and loved.

A FEW NOTES ABOUT THIS STUDY

In each week, I've put all the teaching and questions together, but feel free to divide it up throughout your week as best fits your schedule. There's also a Daily Bible Reading (just one chapter per day) which connects to that week's topic. I encourage you to take three to four minutes each day to make Daily Bible Reading a part of your regular practice instead of doing it all at one time. Each week also includes Scripture Memory, a Prayer Walk (I've included prayer prompts that relate to each week's topic!), and a practical response to what we've learned—we call it the Weekly Challenge. Since we're already leaning into Bible study, I've added these other disciplines to help us build out a more well-rounded spiritual life. Plus, it's just nice to have some variety! The days are numbered each week, but rest assured you can "shuffle the deck" however you need to—the days don't necessarily build on each other. All that to say: the structure is there as a tool. Use it if it's helpful for you, but feel free to disregard it if it isn't.

As you can tell, this study has multiple components. So I've provided a checklist at the beginning of each week to help you organize your Bible study experience. I don't want you to miss anything!

This is a Scripture-heavy study. If you're already familiar with Scripture, my hope is that you'll discover new truths you've never seen before. If you're new to Scripture, I believe you'll feel more equipped and less intimidated to study it by the end of these seven sessions. Some questions will require you to refer to a Greek or Hebrew lexicon, but you don't need to buy one. Plenty of free ones are online. (My favorite is *blueletterbible.org*.)

By the end of this study, you'll be shocked at the dimension and texture and beauty you've started to see in the triune God. It has been there all along—in the Bible we read and the songs we sing—but perhaps we're too familiar with it to notice it. Chances are you're already immersed in the doctrine of the Trinity, so you likely won't have to change any of your beliefs as you read this study; you'll just develop them. They will grow muscles! So will you bring your best to these seven sessions? It will be challenging, but by God's power at work within you, I believe you will come to know and love Him more than you ever thought possible!

INTRODUCTION

#HESWHERETHEJOYIS

1. **DISCUSS the following questions:**

    1. Why are you interested in doing a study about the Trinity?

    2. How would you define the Trinity?

    3. Which Person of the Trinity are you most excited to learn more about? Why?

    4. Based on your current understanding, how would you explain the roles the Persons of the Trinity have played in the story of your salvation? What might be some Bible verses that speak to these roles?

2. **WATCH the Session One video teaching.**

eaching sessions available for purchase
or rent at *lifeway.com/wherethejoyis*

UNITY
&
DIVERSITY

THE WEEK AHEAD

These are the elements of your personal study for the week. Feel free to do them in whatever order works best for your schedule. Check off the items as you move through them.

☐ **DAILY BIBLE READING & PODCAST**

Each day this week you'll read a chapter of Scripture and answer a series of questions to help you reflect on what you read.

☐ Day 1	☐ Day 5
☐ Day 2	☐ Day 6
☐ Day 3	☐ Day 7
☐ Day 4	

☐ **SCRIPTURE MEMORY**

Five days this week you'll work on memorizing 1 John 1:5. Each day you'll find a prompt or easy exercise to help you.

☐ Day 1	☐ Day 4
☐ Day 2	☐ Day 5
☐ Day 3	

☐ **STUDY**

This session's study will lay the foundation for our study of the triune God. You'll get an overview of His character and work, and you'll look at the three foundations of the Trinity. Feel free to work through this content at your own pace.

☐ **WEEKLY CHALLENGE**

The weekly challenge will help you process and respond to what you've studied this week. We encourage you to do this after you've worked through the teaching content.

☐ **PRAYER WALK**

Choose a day this week to prayer walk. We've provided some guidelines to help you structure this time with God.

☐ **GROUP MEETING**

Meet with your group to watch and discuss the video teaching.

1

DAILY BIBLE READING & PODCAST: **GENESIS 1**

 Read the Daily Bible Reading chapter for the day
or listen to the podcast for the day.

Daily Bible Reading Questions:

Where did you see God show up in the text today?

What did you notice about His character or His attributes?

Did you read anything that pointed to what He loves, what
He hates, what He does, or what motivates His actions? If
so, list what you found below.

To access the daily podcast, visit
lifeway.com/wherethejoyis

DAILY BIBLE READING & PODCAST: **EPHESIANS 1**

Read the Daily Bible Reading chapter for the day
or listen to the podcast for the day.

Daily Bible Reading Questions:

Where did you see God show up in the text today?

What did you notice about His character or His attributes?

Did you read anything that pointed to what He loves, what He
hates, what He does, or what motivates His actions? If so, list
what you found below.

DAILY BIBLE READING & PODCAST: **PHILIPPIANS 1**

> 🎤 Read the Daily Bible Reading chapter for the day or listen to the podcast for the day.

Daily Bible Reading Questions:

Where did you see God show up in the text today?

What did you notice about His character or His attributes?

Did you read anything that pointed to what He loves, what He hates, what He does, or what motivates His actions? If so, list what you found below.

SCRIPTURE MEMORY: 1 JOHN 5:1

Today, we begin working on this week's Scripture memory verse. On Days Three through Seven of each week, we'll provide different daily prompts to help you succeed at this. Scripture memory can be challenging, whether this is your first attempt or a regular discipline. But don't underestimate the work God can do in and through you. Commit two to five minutes of your day to memorizing Scripture and watch what happens in just a few days. We gain strength by repetition, so today we'll focus on getting in some reps.

> Everyone who believes that Jesus is the Christ has been born of God, and everyone who loves the Father loves whoever has been born of him.
>
> **1 JOHN 5:1**

Read the verse aloud three times and/or sing along with the verse song if it's helpful.

Write the verse three times in the space provided.

To sing along with the verse song from the podcast, visit *lifeway.com/wherethejoyis*

4

DAILY BIBLE READING & PODCAST: **COLOSSIANS 1**

Read the Daily Bible Reading chapter for the day
or listen to the podcast for the day.

Daily Bible Reading Questions:

Where did you see God show up in the text today?

What did you notice about His character or His attributes?

Did you read anything that pointed to what He loves, what
He hates, what He does, or what motivates His actions? If
so, list what you found below.

SCRIPTURE MEMORY: 1 JOHN 5:1

Everyone who believes that Jesus is the Christ has been born of God, and everyone who loves the Father loves whoever has been born of him.

1 JOHN 5:1

Read the verse aloud three times and/or sing along with the verse song if it's helpful.

Because it's important for us to not only memorize Scripture but to make sure we comprehend it as well, write the verse in your own words.

DAY

DAILY BIBLE READING & PODCAST: **HEBREWS 1**

Read the Daily Bible Reading chapter for the day or listen to the podcast for the day.

Daily Bible Reading Questions:

Where did you see God show up in the text today?

What did you notice about His character or His attributes?

Did you read anything that pointed to what He loves, what He hates, what He does, or what motivates His actions? If so, list what you found below.

SCRIPTURE MEMORY: 1 JOHN 5:1

> Everyone who believes that Jesus is the Christ has been born of God, and everyone who loves the Father loves whoever has been born of him.
>
> **1 JOHN 5:1**

Read the verse aloud three times and/or sing along with the verse song if it's helpful.

Today, let's see what kind of progress you're making with your reps. Cover the verse above and then try to write it from memory in the space provided. You can glance back at it as needed, but be sure to finish each attempt. Keep trying until you're able to write it from start to finish without looking.

6 DAY

DAILY BIBLE READING & PODCAST: **ROMANS 1**

Read the Daily Bible Reading chapter for the day or listen to the podcast for the day.

Daily Bible Reading Questions:

Where did you see God show up in the text today?

What did you notice about His character or His attributes?

Did you read anything that pointed to what He loves, what He hates, what He does, or what motivates His actions? If so, list what you found below.

SCRIPTURE MEMORY: 1 JOHN 5:1

Everyone who believes that Jesus is the Christ has been born of God, and everyone who loves the Father loves whoever has been born of him.

1 JOHN 5:1

Read the verse aloud three times and/or sing along with the verse song if it's helpful.

This verse is packed full of truth! It may be short, but it is dense. Try to discover at least three truths in this verse and write them below.

DAILY BIBLE READING & PODCAST: **ROMANS 8**

Read the Daily Bible Reading chapter for the day
or listen to the podcast for the day.

Daily Bible Reading Questions:

Where did you see God show up in the text today?

What did you notice about His character or His attributes?

Did you read anything that pointed to what He loves, what
He hates, what He does, or what motivates His actions? If
so, list what you found below.

SCRIPTURE MEMORY: 1 JOHN 5:1

Everyone who believes that Jesus is the Christ has been born of God, and everyone who loves the Father loves whoever has been born of him.

1 JOHN 5:1

Read the verse aloud three times and/or sing along with the verse song if it's helpful.

If you enjoy creating, draw a picture in the space provided of what this verse brings to mind visually for you. If you'd rather not draw a picture, write the verse from memory.

GOD'S REVEALING

Have you ever fumbled through your house in a power outage, bumping into walls and bruising your shins on the coffee table? You easily navigate your way around that furniture on a daily basis, but with the lights off, it can be more of a challenge. Many of us who have spent time in church or in Scripture keep bumping into the Trinity but aren't able to identify or describe it clearly. There's a good reason for that. Through most of the Bible, it may seem as though God doesn't say a lot about the Trinity—at least not directly.

I borrowed the darkened house illustration from B. B. Warfield, who said the Old Testament is like a furnished room that is dimly lit, and the New Testament is where God flips on the light switch.[1] This is especially true where the Trinity is concerned. The Trinity "furniture" has been there all along, sitting in the same spots, and the New Testament light just reveals where the furniture has always been.

It's not as though God was being cruel in the Old Testament. He wasn't trying to bruise any shins. He knows relationships work best through progressive revelation, a gradual revealing of more and more information over time. In healthy relationships, we don't expect to share or learn everything the first time we meet someone. This is how Scripture describes God's relationship with humanity. He didn't reveal His whole plan for His people at one time. Instead, He used different means at different times, patiently giving us more information piece by piece as He moved through the process.

These highlighted words can be found in the glossary on page 214.

Despite God's progressive revelation, you and I have most likely suffered from another problem: We've been living in this furnished, lit house while wearing blindfolds. We've bumped into some things here and there; we've sat on them and trusted their ability to hold us up. Perhaps we've even occasionally gotten a glimpse of the room layout when we tilt our heads at just the right angle. But we haven't actively explored what He progressively revealed. Now is the time for us to take our blindfolds off and let the light of Scripture show us the beauty and design of this house we've been living in.

Look through the list of heresies on page 215. Have you ever heard of or encountered any of these? Have you ever believed any of them? If so, which ones? List them below. As we make our way through this study, you'll discover verses that speak truth to the lies you've believed or encountered. When you come across those verses, refer back to the "Heresies" page and make note of the verses beside the heresies they address.

Much of what we know about the Trinity wasn't revealed until the New Testament. In the Old Testament, God's first priority was explaining to His people that He is ONE God—the one true God. Polytheism was rampant among all the other nations, and God wanted to redirect the hearts of His people to the truth, so He repeated this theme throughout the Old Testament. In fact, to both ancient and modern Jews who rely on the Old Testament, the most important Scripture is generally regarded to be Deuteronomy 6:4, "Hear, O Israel: The LORD our God, the LORD is one." God is one. This doctrine stands out as the most important doctrine of the Old Testament, the heart of monotheism (the belief in one God—as opposed to polytheism, the belief in many gods). But this verse points to far more than just the fact that there is one God—it points to His preeminence as the one true God. He is singular in His essence and superior in His being.

Since the ancient Jews were surrounded by polytheistic nations, the Old Testament writers spent a lot of effort establishing there is one true God. Only then could God begin to introduce more complexity about Himself: He is one God who consists of three Persons. In the next steps of His progressive revelation, God sent His Son to earth to dwell among the people and then sent His Spirit to dwell within His people.

Read Hebrews 1:1-3.

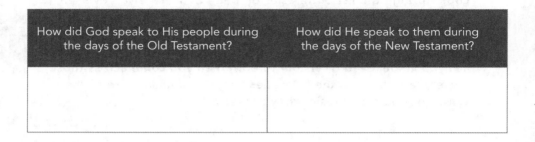

How did God speak to His people during the days of the Old Testament?	How did He speak to them during the days of the New Testament?

God's process remains obscured to someone who only reads the Old Testament. To see the Trinity in the Old Testament, you have to read it through the New Testament lens. But make no mistake: God had been dropping hints about the Trinity since Genesis 1. We'll see some of them in this study.

There's one important thing we must note when it comes to Scripture's progressive revelation: it is not corrective revelation. When God reveals something new, He doesn't negate something He previously revealed. He builds on and expands what He has already revealed. For instance, even in Genesis 1, the first chapter of the Old Testament, we see hints of the Trinity—God's Word and His Spirit were the means God used to do His work of creation. God was doing one work—creating the universe—through what we only later come to understand as His three Persons.

Read Genesis 1:1-2 and then read John 1:1-3.

Which Persons of the Trinity appear to have been present at creation?

Read Genesis 1:26.

Who is speaking here? Who are the "us/our" statements referring to?

In John 1, we find out that Jesus was present in creation, as described in Genesis 1, as was God's Spirit, who "was hovering over the face of the waters" (Gen. 1:2). When the New Testament points to the Spirit, His actions are described with similar fluttering, wind-related words, helping us see He is the same Person who was present and active at creation. The Old and New Testaments work together to help us better understand what God has been saying all along about His presence and activity in our world.

Let's spend some time looking at God's unity as it applies to His oneness and His diversity as it applies to the three Persons of the Trinity.

GOD'S UNITY

The divine nature is really and entirely identical with each of the three persons, all of whom can therefore be called one.[2]

THOMAS AQUINAS

As we move through this study, we'll cover the three foundations of the Trinity multiple times so you'll know them by heart when we finish.

THE FIRST FOUNDATION OF THE TRINITY IS: **THERE IS ONLY ONE GOD.**

The Bible's descriptions of *Elohim* (the name God gives Himself in Gen. 1:1) and His actions set Him apart from all other gods of all other religions.[3] The Old Testament authors repeatedly emphasized the theme of God's superiority and His oneness. These two themes are tied together—not only is our God the one true God who is set apart in power and eternality, but He is ONE God. If there were any other gods on His level, they would have to be eternal like Him and all-powerful like Him, which is functionally impossible—not only because one of them would've had to create the other, but because that would also require one to predate the other.

Look up the following verses. In your Bible, circle the words that point to God's oneness and unity or write them beside the references below.

- **Exodus 20:3**

- **Deuteronomy 6:4-5**

- **Isaiah 43:10**

- **Isaiah 44:24**

- **Isaiah 45:22**

Since progressive revelation isn't corrective, the New Testament reiterates the theme of "one-ness" from the Old Testament, even as it helps understand the three Persons of God.

Read the following verses slowly and carefully and then note the following information beside each reference: What aspects of these passages point to God's unity and oneness? What aspects point to His diversity of Persons?

Verse	What aspects of these passages point to God's unity and oneness?	What aspects point to His diversity of Persons?
Genesis 1:26-27		
Matthew 28:19		
1 Corinthians 8:6		

The fact that we are baptized into only one name, not names (see Matt. 28:19), is significant, especially as it refers collectively to the three Persons of God. In Scripture, a name represents the will, character, and essence of a person. The Trinity has one will, character, and essence across all three divine Persons, even in the Old Testament where the Trinity is less evident.

Consistency

If you've ever studied the Old Testament, you may have come away thinking something along these lines: *Why is God so angry in the Old Testament? I like the New Testament better. God is so much nicer after Jesus shows up on the scene.*

If you've had similar thoughts, you're not alone. I've had them too. But when we pull God and His actions out of context, as we're often prone to do, it's easy to misunderstand His character. If we divide Him into three Persons without remembering He is ONE, we may begin to assign certain temperaments to the Persons of the Trinity (i.e. the Father is the angry one; Jesus is the nice one, and the Spirit is the weird and/or mysterious one). The good news for us (as we will come to see in the pages ahead) is that this is theologically impossible. Much to our relief, "Old Testament God" isn't unlikable as we've believed Him to be. For all of us who have ever felt that way, Scripture is here to set us straight and invite us into something much more beautiful and winsome. Whew!

Contrary to popular thought, God doesn't undergo a personality transplant at the end of the Old Testament. When we follow the storyline of Scripture, we see a God who created mankind out of an overflow of love, who clothed Adam and Eve before they even repented, who rescued the Israelites out of slavery and then led them as they established a functioning society, joyfully choosing to set up camp in their midst and repeatedly forgiving them, blessing them, and reminding them He was sending a Messiah to rescue them. This is the heart of God evident in the scope of the Old Testament's metanarrative. All along He dropped hints of what was coming, and then He delivered on His promise!

Of course, if we drop down in the middle of the Old Testament in a time when He's punishing the Israelites, He seems harsh. We won't understand why His laws were helpful and necessary. We'll fail to notice He's already told them repeatedly not to do that specific sinful thing, told them what type of punishment to expect if/when they do it, and then continued to provide for them and protect them despite their rebellion. With our limited information, we'll view Him as strict or angry, and we won't draw near to Him. We'll prefer to stay in the New Testament where we can read about Jesus, who paid for all the sins we know we've committed. This is a common problem we encounter when we don't read the story of Scripture chronologically (in the order it happened, not the order it is laid out). Reading the Bible at all is great, but reading chronologically can help us get to know God in the order He chose to reveal Himself through progressive revelation.

There is a necessary process of the gospel: we must be confronted with God's laws and requirements, see that we fall short and can't obey His laws, and realize our need for rescue. Jesus came to be that Rescuer—He not only paid our sin debt, but He also granted us His righteousness! This is how progressive revelation works in our relationship with God, and it's the reason we still desperately need the truths of the Old Testament to see Him rightly!

The same is true of our understanding of the Trinity. Without the Old Testament, it might be easy to divide God into three separate Gods, or even to think God shape-shifts from one "form" into the other. (See *Tritheism* and *Modalism* in the list of heresies on p. 215.) But when we read Scripture as a whole, we see His oneness throughout, which helps us maintain this doctrinal balance: *Each Person of the Trinity indwells the other two.* We can't emphasize one Person of God over the others. It's vital to view them holistically, or we'll be led into heresy. But the Trinity doesn't mean God is divided into three parts like pieces of a pie. *Each Person of the Trinity fully possesses/is the complete divine essence.* The word we use to describe this is consubstantial—regarded as the same in substance or essence.

Since they are all equally and fully divine within the Trinity unto themselves, no one Person plays an eternally dominant role. They each point to the others. The Father glorifies and points to the Son. The Son glorifies and points to the Father and the Spirit, and the Spirit glorifies and points to the

Son and the Father. Understanding this truth is VITAL. It shows us so much about God's character. He is always pointing externally—even with Himself. This shows us the heart of God is focused on outgoing love.

The Persons of God aren't only united in their essence, but they're united in their purpose as well. And this divine, eternal unity is inseparable. God has always been One, and He has always been Three. He didn't become this way to serve some kind of purpose or function; it is who He is and how He is.

Recall the first foundation of the Trinity and write it below.

GOD'S DIVERSITY

THE SECOND FOUNDATION OF THE TRINITY IS: **THERE ARE THREE DIVINE PERSONS OF THE ONE TRUE GOD.**

Read Genesis 1:1.

> **Look up *Elohim* (the name God uses for Himself in this verse) in a Hebrew lexicon. What part of speech is it? In what form— singular or plural? What is noteworthy about this?**

In his book *Shared Life*, Donald Macleod said, "The New Testament disclosure of the Father, the Son, and the Holy Spirit is the best, and possibly the only, explanation of God's giving himself a plural name [*Elohim*]" in the Old Testament.[4]

Having a God who is one in nature/being and three in Persons can seem confusing or contradictory, but that's simply because there's nothing else like Him in existence. No other religion in the history of the world has ever had a God like this, and we would do well to learn about Him since He's the foundation of our faith.

Not long after God flipped the lights on in the New Testament, Christians began trying to find ways to summarize and explain this doctrine. As we discussed in "A Word from the Author," all analogies sacrifice some aspect of who He is and lead us to one or more heresies we discussed in the Introduction. (See p. 215.) As complex as the Trinity may be, you and I benefit personally from the fact that God is both One and triune. So we won't simplify His complexity; we'll study it. After all, stained glass windows are more captivating because of their many panes and colors. Diamonds are more brilliant and valuable as their facets increase. God's complexity adds to His beauty, and not only does He invite us into His mysteries, but He offers wisdom if we ask Him (Jas. 1:5), and He shares His secrets with His friends (Ps. 25:14)—and that's you!

THE THIRD FOUNDATION OF THE TRINITY IS: **THE THREE PERSONS ARE COEQUAL, CO-ETERNAL, AND CO-RELATIONAL.**

God is one essence (or nature) and three Persons: The Father, Son, and Spirit are all equally and fully God, and "the being of each Person is equal to the whole being of God."[5] They're not only equal in character and personality, but in power, glory, and eternality. Since they're all co-eternal, that means none of them were created by the others. This is important, and it's one of the places where our modern, Western mindset often fails us because we're tempted to attach ages to their names.

We think of a father as one who comes before a son and who played a role in creating that son and who must be separate from the son even though they share some DNA. But in the eternal Godhead, the name *Father* points to One who gives His identity to another person; He is the Unbegotten and the Begetter. The "Son" is the One who displays that identity. Hebrews 5:5 describes Jesus as being "begotten" of the Father, which conveys the idea of the Father appointing the Son, not creating Him. To prevent any confusion about this, theologians often use the phrase "eternally begotten" to describe Jesus (John 1:1-18). As for the Spirit, Jesus described Him as the One who "proceeds from" the Father (John 15:26), and there's also evidence He proceeds from the Son (John 16:7). While we may not understand this fully, Scripture helps us understand it better.

These descriptions of appointing, sending, begetting, and proceeding tell us a lot about the Trinity: they're united in their mission, and they have distinct roles as they engage with us in that mission.

> While the three members of the Trinity are distinct, this does not mean that any is inferior to the other. Instead, they are all identical in attributes. They are equal in power, love, mercy, justice, holiness, knowledge, and all other qualities. Each Person is fully God.[6]
>
> **MATT PERMAN**

Since they are co-eternal and coequal Persons on a united mission, it's vital for us to remember that one of them isn't more important than the other. In his book *Forgotten Trinity*, James R. White described it like this: "Just because the Father, Son, and Spirit do different things does not mean that any one of them is inferior to the others in nature. Think of it this way: in eternity past, the Father, Son, and Spirit voluntarily and freely chose the roles they would take in bringing about the redemption of God's people . . . Each took different roles of necessity."[7]

Look up the following verses. In your Bible, circle each reference (including nouns and pronouns) to a Person of the Trinity—or write them beside the verses below. Note: in these verses, *God* usually refers to the Father.
- **Matthew 28:19**
- **Luke 10:21**
- **2 Corinthians 1:21-22**
- **2 Corinthians 13:14 (v. 13 in the CSB translation)**
- **Ephesians 3:14**

It's common to refer to the Persons of God in this order: the Father is the first Person of God; the Son is the second Person of God; and the Spirit is the third Person of God. But it's important to note that this order doesn't mean one Person is older or more important than the others. Instead, this order points to God's progressive revelation in Scripture and in relationship with us.

You may wonder why this has to be so complex. Why can't He just be "God" and let that be all we need to know? In his book *The Deep Things of God*, Fred Sanders said,

> God's way of being God is to be Father, Son, and Holy Spirit simultaneously from all eternity, perfectly complete in a triune fellowship of love. If we don't take this as our starting point, everything we say about the practical relevance of the Trinity could lead us to one colossal misunderstanding: thinking of God the Trinity as a means to some other end.[8]

If we preferred worshiping the version of Him we've imagined instead of getting to know who He really is, we'd be guilty of idolatry at worst and laziness at best. And on top of that, we'd be missing out on some of the most beautiful aspects of who He is and the joy that comes from knowing Him more!

There are things we can't see about Him if we don't look closely at His tri-unity. For instance, if God were unipersonal instead of triune, He couldn't be love in His essence. It would be something He does, not something He is because He wouldn't have been capable of love until He created something to love. Love requires an "other." That means He would've been Creator before He was Love, and His love would be attached to His accomplishments. But since He has always been a community of love within Himself, then love is at the core of who He is. He has always been other-oriented. God faces outward. Tim Keller said this means that "love is cosmic ultimate reality." Keller goes on to explain that without the Trinity, the ultimate reality of love falls apart.[9] For instance, polytheists worship gods who are contending for power, not love. In eastern religions, where god is merely a force, their god is impersonal and can't contain love, be love, or give love.

One of the ways we see the love within the Godhead (another name for the Trinity), is when they talk to or about each other. This happens most often in the New Testament. In the Gospels, we get to eavesdrop on Jesus' prayer life where He talks directly to the Father, and we also hear Him describing the work of the Holy Spirit to His disciples. These conversations reveal not only that Father, Son, and Holy Spirit are three distinct Persons, but that they're each focused on the others, deferring to them and pointing toward their glory out of their love for each other. It becomes clear that they aim to glorify each other.

Look up the verses below then answer the following questions for each verse: Who is speaking? Who is the speaker speaking to or about? Why? (You may need to read the surrounding context to find answers.)

Verse	Who is speaking?	Who is He speaking to or about?	Why?
Matthew 3:17			
Matthew 17:5			
Luke 22:42			
John 14:26			
John 14:31			
John 16:7			
John 17:24			

Recall the second foundation of the Trinity and write it below.

Recall the third foundation of the Trinity and write it below.

GOD'S RELATIONSHIPS

In the previous section, we saw how much the Trinity loves each other, points to each other, and glorifies each other. Their actions are motivated by love! And because this is all built on and fueled by perfect love, that means there is deep, abiding, gospel joy at the heart of the Trinity. That joy is not just contained within God Himself—it's joy for us too!

God is inherently relational. In this section, we'll look at two general categories of God's relationships: His relationship within the Trinity and His relationship with humanity.

What we've been talking about up to this point is primarily God's relationship within Himself—the Father, the Son, and the Spirit. This internal life of God is what theologians often refer to as the Immanent Trinity because *immanent* means "existing or operating within; inherent."[10] (Note: Some theologians prefer to use the term *Ontological Trinity* instead of *Immanent Trinity*. Both titles refer to the same thing.)

This term points to all the things we've covered in the previous sections about how God operates within Himself, the inner life of the divine community of the Father, Son, and Spirit. "God is love" within Himself.

Even though we all love hearing about ourselves, it's important that we cover this relationship first because, as Fred Sanders said, "God is Trinity primarily for himself and only secondarily for us."[11] If that comes as a shock or a surprise, hang in there—we'll eventually see why this is not only important but comforting. It would be wrong to think of ourselves as God's primary focal point and purpose; that is not the message of Scripture.

The closer we lean in to see Him, the more we'll discover about Him and the more His joy will embed itself into our lives. He created us and invited us into a preexisting joy. Scripture never tells us why God created the world and mankind, but it does tell us what God was doing before He made us. For all eternity, He has been and is and will be reveling in infinite communal love, which means God is infinitely happy! If God were singular, His reasons for creating the world would've been rooted in need, boredom, loneliness, or power—all of which would point to His selfishness in creating. Instead, He was already fulfilled in His triune perfection.

Read John 17:24.

Circle the word that points to God's pre-creation action or note it below.

What was God doing before He created the world? Love. And this wasn't a one-way love; the Persons of God point outside themselves to each other as a result of love.

Look up the following verses (and their context) and then fill in the blank to show who was glorifying/pointing to whom:

John 16:13-15

_____ will glorify Jesus.

_____ will declare the words of _____.

The words of Jesus are from _____.

Look up the following verses (and their context) and then fill in the blank to show who was glorifying/pointing to whom:

John 17:4-5

Jesus glorified ⬚⬚⬚⬚⬚⬚⬚⬚⬚⬚⬚⬚ .

Jesus asked ⬚⬚⬚⬚⬚⬚⬚⬚⬚ to glorify Him.

If humans were God's focal point, He would be unfulfilled without us, which means He wouldn't be infinitely happy. We very much want and need a happy God, so it's good news for us that He is! Fred Sanders said, "The boundless life that God lives in himself, at home, within the happy land of the Trinity above all worlds, is perfect. It is complete, inexhaustibly full, and infinitely blessed."[12] We see this emphasized in Scripture's teachings of the early church as well.

Read Acts 17:24-25.

According to that passage, what does God need? What needs God? Why?

God needs nothing. That's why He can love so well. This is the best hint we have about why God would create the world—out of an overflow of His infinite love and happiness!

This brings us to the second category of God's relationships; it's something theologians often refer to as the Economic Trinity. The word *economic* comes from the Greek word *oikonomia*, which means *household management*.[13] This phrase essentially relates to how the triune God works outside of Himself, and more specifically, within His family. (That's us!) It refers to all the ways God's personal love spills out into the world.

Before we move deeper into this, let's summarize the internal/external relationships of the Trinity.

Immanent Trinity (internal relationships that pertain to being)

- The Father is the Father because He eternally begets the Son.

- The Son is the Son because He is eternally begotten of the Father.

- The Spirit is the Spirit because He eternally proceeds from the Father, through the Son.

Economic Trinity (external relationships that pertain to doing)

- The Father sent the Son.

- The Son is sent by/of the Father.

- The Spirit is sent by/of the Father and the Son.

These details undergird everything else we'll cover in this study. We will spend time focusing on specific ways the Economic Trinity engages with humanity, but it's important to remember that everything God does flows from who He is, not the other way around. "Trinity" is not the work uniform He puts on when He deals with humanity; it's who He has always been throughout all eternity, unchanged.

You're probably already familiar with some of the major aspects of God's external work—it includes creation, salvation, and restoration. We tend to assign certain works to certain Persons of the Trinity—we think of the Father as the One who created the world, the Son as the One who saved us, etc.— but Scripture reveals that each Person of the Trinity is active in the whole process. While they each have unique roles, they have one shared goal and are each vital in God's relationship with His children.

Read 1 Peter 1:1-2.

What role did Peter attribute to each of the Persons of God in the process of adopting these people into His family?

Father	
Spirit	
Son	

Fred Sanders frequently reiterates in his writings, "The Trinity is the gospel."[14] Without the active engagement of any one of them in our lives, our rescue would fall apart. Inasmuch as they all point to each other and seek to glorify each other in their unity, they work together to pour that love out toward us. The cross demonstrates the infinite loving heart of God to us. It shows us who God has been all along, independent of us. This is why it's so important that God's triune nature is first for Him and secondarily for us. Since we have a God who is already completely fulfilled within Himself, He delights to share that unity and joy! "If this is true," Tim Keller said, "then your absolute highest purpose, your meaning, and the only way you'll ever be happy is if you are glorifying God above all other things."[15] As we seek to live for God's glory, we'll get the joy and delight that comes as a result.

Has there been a time when you actively tried to glorify God in your actions, not out of pressure or guilt, but out of joy? If so, describe that experience and/or the kind of thoughts that came to mind at the time.

Think of a time when you've actively disregarded God and sought to glorify yourself instead. Describe that experience and/or the kinds of thoughts that came to mind at the time.

Love is inherent to who God is. That's what He has extended to us and invited us into. He wants joy for you, and that's why He draws you near—because He's where the joy is!

The Weekly Challenge is our practical response to what we've learned in our study and in God's Word this week.

This week we learned that love is at the very core of God's nature. He has always been acting in love—toward Himself and toward you! Since we all want to feel loved, pray and ask Him to give you eyes to recognize His love for you in the various ways it shows up. Throughout this week, be attentive to the ways you feel and see His love for you, trying to identify at least one way each day. Note your experience on your phone, in your journal, or below. Thank God for those glimpses of His character and His relationship with you.

> Give thanks to the God of heaven, for his
>
> steadfast love endures forever.
>
> **PSALM 136:26**

If you're the artistic type, you might even want to create a painting or write a song about the ways you see His love show up in your life.

If weather and health permit, take a thirty-minute prayer walk. If you're unable to go for a walk, try to find a place outside or a quiet spot in your home where you can sit and talk with God. Use the following prompts to guide your prayer time. Silence your phone and set a recurring timer for every ten minutes. Each prompt represents a ten-minute segment of prayer.

 Section A (Minutes 1–10): Praise God for who He is and what He does (Ps. 136:26). Thank Him for anything He has taught you about Himself this week. Thank Him for the blessings He has brought into your life.

 Section B (Minutes 11–20): Ask God to search your heart and reveal any of your sinful thoughts, words, attitudes, or actions. Confess your sin to Him when He reveals it to you. Because Jesus has already paid your sin debt, there is no shame in these confessions—only freedom and peace (Rom. 8:1-3). Ask Him to turn your heart from sin and turn it toward Himself instead.

 Section C (Minutes 21–30): Talk to God about any of your needs or wants (Matt. 7:11). He invites us to bring both the big things and the small things to Him. He already knows what's on your heart and mind, but He wants you to share it with Him in conversation.

GROUP MEETING

1. **OPEN** with a time of greeting and prayer.

2. **REVIEW** your work from this week:
   - ☐ Scripture Memory
   - ☐ Weekly Challenge
   - ☐ Prayer Walk

3. **WATCH** the Session Two teaching video and use the space below to jot down any notes.

_____

_____

_____

_____

_____

_____

_____

_____

_____

_____

_____

_____

_____

_____

_____

_____

_____

Teaching sessions available for purchase or rent at *lifeway.com/wherethejoyis*

4. DISCUSS your personal study from last week and today's teaching video using the following questions:

The three foundations of the Trinity are:
1. There is only one God.
2. There are three divine Persons of the one true God.
3. The three Persons are coequal, co-eternal, and co-relational.

Have you ever struggled to believe any of these foundations? If so, was this session helpful for you? Explain.

What heresies have you encountered or believed? After this week's study, do you have a firmer grasp on why they're inaccurate? Explain.

How did the study this week help you come to a greater understanding of God's character as being consistent throughout Scripture?

How do we benefit from the fact that God is a triune God instead of a solitary god? How would a solitary god be different?

Fred Sanders said, "God is Trinity primarily for himself and only secondarily for us."[16] What did you think about this quote when you first read it? Was it offensive to you? If so, why?

How did your understanding of that quote shift, if at all, after completing this week's personal study?

How would you describe the differences between the Immanent Trinity and the Economic Trinity?

What was your favorite takeaway from this week's study? How will it impact the way you live this week?

5. CLOSE with prayer.

session three

GOD THE
FATHER

#HESWHERETHEJOYIS

THE WEEK AHEAD ───────────────

These are the elements of your personal study for the week. Feel free to do them in whatever order works best for your schedule. Check off the items as you move through them.

☐ **DAILY BIBLE READING & PODCAST**

Each day this week you'll read a chapter of Scripture and answer a series of questions to help you reflect on what you read.

☐ Day 1   ☐ Day 5

☐ Day 2   ☐ Day 6

☐ Day 3   ☐ Day 7

☐ Day 4

☐ **SCRIPTURE MEMORY**

Five days this week you'll work on memorizing 1 John 5:2. Each day you'll find a prompt or easy exercise to help you.

☐ Day 1   ☐ Day 4

☐ Day 2   ☐ Day 5

☐ Day 3

☐ **STUDY**

Your study this session will focus on the first Person of the Trinity, God the Father. You'll examine His role in creation and redemption and better understand His character and His actions.

☐ **WEEKLY CHALLENGE**

The weekly challenge will help you process and respond to what you've studied this week. We encourage you to do this after you've worked through the teaching content.

☐ **PRAYER WALK**

Choose a day this week to prayer walk. We've provided some guidelines to help you structure this time with God.

☐ **GROUP MEETING**

Meet with your group to watch and discuss the teaching video.

DAY **1**

DAILY BIBLE READING & PODCAST: **JOHN 1**

Read the Daily Bible Reading chapter for the day or listen to the podcast for the day.

Daily Bible Reading Questions:

Where did you see God show up in the text today?

What did you notice about His character or His attributes?

Did you read anything that pointed to what He loves, what He hates, what He does, or what motivates His actions? If so, list what you found below.

To access the daily podcast, visit
lifeway.com/wherethejoyis

DAILY BIBLE READING & PODCAST: **JOHN 2**

> Read the Daily Bible Reading chapter for the day
> or listen to the podcast for the day.

Daily Bible Reading Questions:

Where did you see God show up in the text today?

What did you notice about His character or His attributes?

Did you read anything that pointed to what He loves, what He hates, what He does, or what motivates His actions? If so, list what you found below.

DAILY BIBLE READING & PODCAST: **JOHN 3**

Read the Daily Bible Reading chapter for the day
or listen to the podcast for the day.

Daily Bible Reading Questions:

Where did you see God show up in the text today?

What did you notice about His character or His attributes?

Did you read anything that pointed to what He loves, what
He hates, what He does, or what motivates His actions? If
so, list what you found below.

SCRIPTURE MEMORY: 1 JOHN 5:2

Today, we start memorizing our next verse. We'll provide different daily prompts on Days Three through Seven of each week to help you succeed at this. Since we're memorizing cumulatively—that is, adding to what we learn each week instead of replacing it—we will occasionally recall verses from previous weeks. We gain strength by repetition, so today we'll focus on getting in some reps!

> By this we know that we love the children of God, when we love God and obey his commandments.
>
> **1 JOHN 5:2**

Read the verse aloud three times and/or sing along with the verse song if it's helpful.

Write the verse three times in the space provided.

Recite the cumulative verses from both sessions (1 John 5:1-2) aloud three times.

To sing along with the verse song from the podcast, visit *lifeway.com/wherethejoyis*

4

DAY

DAILY BIBLE READING & PODCAST: JOHN 4

Read the Daily Bible Reading chapter for the day or listen to the podcast for the day.

Daily Bible Reading Questions:

Where did you see God show up in the text today?

What did you notice about His character or His attributes?

Did you read anything that pointed to what He loves, what He hates, what He does, or what motivates His actions? If so, list what you found below.

SCRIPTURE MEMORY: 1 JOHN 5:1-2

Everyone who believes that Jesus is the Christ has been born of God, and everyone who loves the Father loves whoever has been born of him. By this we know that we love the children of God, when we love God and obey his commandments.

1 JOHN 5:1-2

Read the verses aloud three times and/or sing along with the verse song if it's helpful.

Because it's important for us to not only memorize Scripture but to make sure we comprehend it as well, write our new verse for this week, 1 John 5:2, in your own words.

DAY 5

DAILY BIBLE READING & PODCAST: **JOHN 5**

Read the Daily Bible Reading chapter for the day
or listen to the podcast for the day.

Daily Bible Reading Questions:

Where did you see God show up in the text today?

What did you notice about His character or His attributes?

Did you read anything that pointed to what He loves, what
He hates, what He does, or what motivates His actions? If so,
list what you found below.

SCRIPTURE MEMORY: 1 JOHN 5:1-2

Everyone who believes that Jesus is the Christ has been born of God, and everyone who loves the Father loves whoever has been born of him. By this we know that we love the children of God, when we love God and obey his commandments.

1 JOHN 5:1-2

Read the verses aloud three times and/or sing along with the verse song if it's helpful.

Today, let's see what kind of progress we're making with our reps. Cover the verses above and then try to write them both from memory. You can glance back if you need to, but be sure to finish each attempt. Keep trying until you're able to write it from start to finish without looking.

DAY 6

DAILY BIBLE READING & PODCAST: JOHN 6

🎙 Read the Daily Bible Reading chapter for the day or listen to the podcast for the day.

Daily Bible Reading Questions:

Where did you see God show up in the text today?

What did you notice about His character or His attributes?

Did you read anything that pointed to what He loves, what He hates, what He does, or what motivates His actions? If so, list what you found below.

SCRIPTURE MEMORY: 1 JOHN 5:1-2

Everyone who believes that Jesus is the Christ has been born of God, and everyone who loves the Father loves whoever has been born of him. By this we know that we love the children of God, when we love God and obey his commandments.

1 JOHN 5:1-2

Read the verses aloud three times and/or sing along with the verse song if it's helpful.

Try to discover at least three truths in 1 John 5:2 and write them below.

DAY

DAILY BIBLE READING & PODCAST: JOHN 7

Read the Daily Bible Reading chapter for the day or listen to the podcast for the day.

Daily Bible Reading Questions:

Where did you see God show up in the text today?

What did you notice about His character or His attributes?

Did you read anything that pointed to what He loves, what He hates, what He does, or what motivates His actions? If so, list what you found below.

SCRIPTURE MEMORY: 1 JOHN 5:1-2

> Everyone who believes that Jesus is the Christ has been born of God, and everyone who loves the Father loves whoever has been born of him. By this we know that we love the children of God, when we love God and obey his commandments.
>
> **1 JOHN 5:1-2**

Read the verses aloud three times and/or sing along with the verse song if it's helpful.

If you enjoy creating, draw a picture in the space provided of what this verse brings to mind visually for you. If you'd rather not draw a picture, write the verse from memory.

WHY "FATHER"?

Recall the three foundations of the Trinity and write them below.

When you hear the word *father*, how do you internally respond? Does the word have a good or bad connotation? What people and experiences have contributed to your view?

Some of the best men and women I know had terrible fathers. Maybe yours was terrible too or even altogether absent. If that's your story, you may have a hard time warming up to God the Father. You may feel more affinity toward Jesus or the Spirit, preferring to keep the Father at a distance. Even if your earthly father was good, his imperfections might skew your view of the heavenly Father.

So why would God choose the word *Father* for Himself? There were certainly other options. Why didn't He opt for a term that doesn't carry so much baggage? Wouldn't we all prefer "God the Grandmother Who Gives Us Unlimited Ice Cream"? I'm inclined to think God had a redemption story up His sleeve here—as He always does when it comes to His kids. Not only was He the good Father before all our other fathers got it wrong, but He's the One who enters into all the voids they've left behind. Only He knows how to father us perfectly. Because He's our only chance to see what a father should be, I don't want us to miss it! If you're especially hesitant about this session, it's your heart I'm asking Him to speak to the most. I believe He has good things in store for you on the pages of this session.

In Session Two, we learned that the Persons of the Trinity are consubstantial—they have the same essence, and each fully possesses/is the divine essence. So when we see the character of Jesus or the Spirit revealed to us, we also see what the Father is like. If you're drawn to Jesus or the Spirit but you struggle with the Father, let this set your heart at ease: they are revealing Him to you. What you find lovely about each of them is also in Him.

In a patrilineal society—cultures where the father's line is what connects each subsequent generation—the one who gives identity to another person is known as a "father." Both fathers and mothers contribute to the identities of their offspring, but God has specifically chosen to identify Himself as Father, not Mother—though not because He is male. (Since He doesn't have a physical body, He can't be male in the sense that we think of it.) But in this patrilineal society, "Father" gives us the best understanding of the role He plays not only toward us but toward the other Persons of the Trinity as well. The Father is Father because He eternally begets and loves the Son.

Just as you want to be called by your name, we honor God by thinking of Him as Father and calling Him Father; it's consistent with what He has told us about who He is, and He cannot lie. Addressing God this way doesn't just honor Him, it's a huge honor to us too! The fact that the God of the Universe invites sinful humans to refer to Him as "Father" is remarkable! He delights to be in a relationship with us. He doesn't turn His nose up at us or roll His eyes; He calls us His beloved children.

> For if God is not a Father, if he has no Son and will have no
> children, then he must be lonely, distant and unapproachable; if
> he is not triune and so not essentially loving, then no God at all
> just looks better.[1]
> **MICHAEL REEVES**

Without Him Fathering within the Trinity first, there would be no us. Without a relational triune God, there would be no overflow of love, no catalyst for creation. His being corresponds to His doing. Because in eternity past, the Father, Son, and Spirit have always been who they will always eternally be, their roles for their relationship with humanity follow their identities. For the Father, those roles include being the initiator, the architect of creation. We recognize Jesus' death on the cross as the greatest act of love the world has ever known—and it is—but that monumental event that serves as the foundation of our faith was part of the Father's plan. There's nothing the Son or the Spirit did or do that isn't somehow anchored in the Father's planning and initiation. They do nothing apart from Him.

Look up the following verses and circle the words and phrases in your Bible (or write them by the verses below) that point to Christ's dependence on the Father's will and plan:

Matthew 26:39	
John 4:34	
John 5:19	
John 5:30	
John 6:38	
John 8:28	
1 John 4:14	

The Father's good plan and generous will are connected to every good thing we experience with the Son and the Spirit. He's far more winsome and compassionate than the reputation we sometimes give Him via misinformation we've received or our own misperception. In order to help us understand the Father better and gain perspective on His words and actions, we'll spend the rest of this session looking at who He is, what He's like, and what He does. This order is important because actions are born out of who someone is and what that person is like, but as we look at each section in detail, we'll see lots of overlap since "being" and "doing" are so interwoven. We'll start by looking at the first relationships He ever had, the first relationships to ever exist: the Father within the Trinity.

THE FATHER IN RELATIONSHIP (WHO HE IS)

> When evangelicals lose their sense of proportion, they
> begin to talk as if they no longer care about the character
> of God unless they get something from it. The best defense
> against this has always been the doctrine of the eternal
> Trinity in itself.[2]
> **FRED SANDERS**

Creation is where we first see the roles of the Trinity emerging. But before God took any direct action toward creating humanity, He existed in all of His perfection and glory. He needed nothing, and the fullness of His triune nature dwelled together in perfect love. Out of the overflow of that love, God the Father set His plan in motion to create us and establish a relationship with us.

Creating is the first way we see Him taking action in Scripture, but that's because this is where we enter the story. Of course, God's story began long before ours did. He was fully God before He made anything. It's important to note that His God-ness isn't contingent upon Him being the Creator; otherwise, He wouldn't have been God until the moment when He created. His position as Deity would have relied on causing us to exist. In that sense, He would need us in order to be who He is. But He is dependent on nothing, and everything is dependent on Him. Even before time began, the Father has always been the Father.

In Session Two, we looked at John 17:24 and noted what God was doing before creation. Reread that verse and record why His action was noteworthy.

Before there was ever a creation or a command, there was a Father and His love. He has always loved the Son and the Spirit. The fact that the Father has been loving perfectly for all eternity tells us a lot about who He is. Whenever Scripture peels back the curtain on eternity, we see a glimpse of His great love and His plan to demonstrate that love.

Revelation 13:8 is another verse that shows us what God was doing before He created the earth. What does it reveal?

This passage, along with John 17:24, shows us that the Father was loving perfectly within the Trinity and making plans and provision for His children before the earth was founded. What does that reveal about His character?

If we only see God as Creator and not as Father, we miss out on the relational aspect that God called us to and created us for. We become a product, and He becomes nothing more than our distant, uncaring producer who has moved on to other projects.

But on the other hand, If we see God as only Father, without seeing Him through the lens of the fullness of the triune God, there's a good chance we'll become legalists, especially if we attach our understanding of Him to the experiences we've had with our earthly fathers. We may try to do all the right things to please the Father out of fear of punishment. We have to rightly understand who we're in this relationship with by seeing Him as He exists within the Trinity. To do that, we have to start before the beginning. In other words: we cannot get ourselves right until we get Him right. And we cannot get Him right until we get Them right.

Our origin story starts not only with God the Father but with the eternal triune God, existing in perfect love and unity before the foundation of the world. God created us out of relationship, for relationship. "Then God said, 'Let us make man in our image, after our likeness.' . . . So God created man in his own image, in the image of God he created him; male and female he created them" (Gen. 1:26-27). You exist to be loved by God and to be so moved by His love for you that you love Him in return (1 John 4:19).

What is the difference between seeing God as Creator and seeing God as Father?

Read John 14:6; Romans 15:16-17; and Titus 3:3-7.

What is the only way God the Father can be our Father?

According to Scripture, the only way we can approach the Father as our Father is through the finished work of God the Son and the presence of the Spirit. They always work in unison because, as the second foundation of the Trinity reminds us, there can be no separation. Our salvation and adoption into God's family is the work of all three Persons of the Trinity.

This is an important distinction: while God is the Creator of all creation, He is not the Father of all creation. He is the Father even if He had never created. All humans are His image-bearers and His creation, but the only way we become His children is by adoption into His family. In His great kindness, He adopts some of humanity into His family to be coheirs with His Son Jesus. If we misunderstand how we become God's children, we risk losing sight of the gospel. We only have God as our Father when we repent, place our faith in Christ, and are changed by the Spirit. This occurs when we see the need for His work in our lives. We must recognize our desperation. Jesus referred to this as being "poor in spirit" and He called it a blessing (Matt. 5:3). In modern terms, we might call this *spiritual poverty*— it's the awareness that we have nothing to offer God, which leads us to Jesus. When we acknowledge Jesus as Savior and Lord and receive the Holy Spirit, we're made part of God's family!

Read John 8:42-44.

According to Jesus' words, if someone is not a child of God, who is that person's father? Is this a new idea for you? Is it challenging to accept? Why or why not?

When Jesus paid our sin debt, He not only took on our sins, but He granted us His righteousness. And when we receive Christ, we receive His perfect righteousness, which makes us fit for God's family.

Look up John 1:12.

What is the requirement for being adopted into God's family to become a child of God?

As a sign of our adoption and a "seal" of His approval, the Father sends His Spirit to live in us (Eph. 1:13). When that happens, our relationship with the Father is fixed forever, and we bear His name, just as an adopted child takes on the adoptive family name.

> If you want to judge how well a person understands Christianity, find out how much he makes of the thought of being God's child, and having God as his Father. If this is not the thought that prompts and controls his worship and prayers and his whole outlook on life, it means that he does not understand Christianity very well at all.[3]
>
> **J. I. PACKER**

THE FATHER'S CHARACTER (HOW HE IS)

Performing religious actions without having an affection for God is similar to a loveless marriage. If God's interaction with us was just Him ruling over us, He would only want obedience. But because He is a personal, relational God, He wants to love and be loved. Jonathan Edwards said, "True religion, in a great measure, consists in holy affections."[4] We've been invited into the most beautiful relationship a human could ever know, but we will miss the sheer delight of it all if we view Him wrongly.

Do you find delight in God? If not, can you think of a time when you did? Describe it.

What fears or desires have kept you from drawing nearer to God?

God spends the whole story of Scripture revealing Himself to us. Scripture is not primarily our "to do" list; it is our "to behold" list. We come to Scripture to look for God—what He loves; what He hates; who He is; what motivates Him to do what He does. When we pay attention to what's revealed, we see He's a God who loves and whose wrath and justice abide perfectly with that love. These characteristics aren't in conflict with each other; they work in unison. How so? We all hate anything that threatens the things we love. We want to protect what we love. And that's how God works too. He wants to protect us from harm because He loves us.

We've already established that God is love within Himself, the Trinity, so we know God loves God. That is right and good because He is nothing less than perfectly lovely. Scripture tells us God also loves us, His children. First John 3:1a says, "See what kind of love the Father has given to us, that we should be called children of God; and so we are." Since God loves God and God loves His kids, He lays out some Fatherly, protective rules for us.

God first began making His laws known in the garden of Eden. Adam and Eve only had one law (Gen. 2:17), and the enemy used that one law to prompt them to wonder if God really had their best interests at heart. They doubted Him based on one law. From the start, we see humanity didn't understand who God is; they perceived Him to be cruel. When they sinned, they hid from Him. They didn't believe His love, so they were driven by fear. After all, God had said that on the day they broke His law, they would die. But, shockingly, when God pursued them, He didn't kill them. He clothed them. Even their sin revealed His love for them. But in some ways, the day they sinned, they did die—they lost the kind of life God intended for humanity. Their eventual physical deaths were symptomatic of the curse of being cut off from God's special presence. Romans 5:12 makes it clear that Adam's sin brought about death—physical and eternal—for all of us. But God's response to their sin, and ours, was redemption. He exemplified it (Gen. 3:21) and pointed toward it (Gen. 3:15).

As we move further into the Old Testament, we encounter the Israelites, God's people. They'd been enslaved for four hundred years. By the time God set them free, they had no reason to trust authority. They'd never lived in a free society and had no idea how to keep order. God gave them instructions—commandments—for building a healthy society. He established laws to help them honor Him and others so they could flourish. But they couldn't keep the laws. Did God smite them or give up on them? No. He set up camp—literally—amid a bunch of sinners to live with them!

Forty years after God moved them from slavery in Egypt to freedom in the wilderness, He moved them again—into the promised land. With all the new opportunities at hand, He gave them more information on how to live in their new land (Deut. 7:1-5), how important it was for them to obey His commands (Deut. 11), and how to honor their new kings and each other (Deut. 17:14-20). But still, they resisted. All along, God told them their failure to keep His laws would lead to the downfall of their society. And despite God's mercy and great patience, that's what happened. Their continued disobedience led to devastation and exile.

When it comes to understanding God, here's our problem: if we drop down in the middle of this story, it can seem like "Old Testament God" is harsh and demanding. We wonder which laws apply to us and which we can sidestep without angering Him. If that's the case, we've lost the plot. This is a love story—a story about flourishing and joy! We have to zoom out to remember that this story was set in motion by our great initiating God who was motivated by the overflow of His love. And He wants to be loved back (Matt. 22:36-40). He has a plan to build a relationship with people. That alone is shocking because He's perfect ("complete") and holy ("set apart"), and we are not. We are broken people who never miss an opportunity to do the wrong thing. Yet He leans in; He doesn't run from us or turn His back.

Do you know how I know we've lost the plot? The Israelites, sinful as they were, showed a pattern of rejoicing when God gave them commands. Psalm 119 is the longest chapter in the Bible, and the whole thing is a tribute to God's laws and His kindness in giving them His laws. Why are our responses so different from the original audience?

In Egypt, and in their new land, the Israelites were surrounded by a bunch of pagans who worshiped a variety of gods—some of which they made by hand and others they attached to things like the sun or the weather. This meant the pagans had no idea how to please their gods. They were left guessing. They tried sacrificing their children, cutting themselves, having sex with animals—you name it. They had no instruction manual, no true prophets to guide them.

So when God showed up and reintroduced Himself to His people, His requirements were a great act of kindness to them. What a relief! He told them how and why things worked the way they did in their relationship with Him. He also said they were going to get it all terribly wrong, but that in His kindness, He had already made a way to set things right. From the beginning, He dropped breadcrumbs throughout the Old Testament that pointed to Jesus. In fact, Jesus confirmed that the Old Testament testified about Him (Luke 24:25-27; John 5:39-40).

Only in seeing God rightly can we learn to see ourselves rightly. As we look at Him, we'll inevitably see that we fall short of His standards. All our sin accrues a debt we could never pay. Every doubt, every mixed motive, every selfish thought and word—it all earns us punishment and separation from God. It's what we deserve (Rom. 3:10-20,23). But the sacrifice of Jesus has made a way for us. When we turn from our sin and turn to Him in faith, we find forgiveness.

One of the most beautiful paradoxes in Scripture is where God's utter holiness (set-apart-ness) meets His relentless pursuit of sinners. It's shocking to read the whole story and see that He never stopped wanting to be near those sinners, including you and me! He has united Himself to us inextricably through Christ, and this union is our greatest freedom and our deepest joy!

THE FATHER'S ACTIONS (WHAT HE DOES)

> Since God is, before all things, a Father, and not primarily Creator or Ruler, all his ways are beautifully fatherly. It is not that this God "does" being Father as a day job, only to kick back in the evenings as plain old "God." It is not that he has a nice blob of fatherly icing on top. He is Father. All the way down. Thus all that he does he does as Father.[5]
> **MICHAEL REEVES**

In this section, we'll look specifically at the work God the Father has done in the story of our redemption. One of the challenging parts about these sessions on the individual Persons of the Trinity is that it's impossible to divide the work of God up from Person to Person. They're all collectively engaged in each aspect of their work with humanity. However, they each serve different roles in that work.

As the authority (which comes from the same root as "author") in the Economic Trinity, the Father is the initiator of all good things we experience (Jas. 1:17). He initiated the universe. He initiated mankind. He initiated a relationship with us. He is the One who set all these things in motion. He delights to pursue us out of love, and we'll find our deepest joy in trusting and responding to His love as it reaches out to us through all His actions!

> All God does in relation to His children is done as Father. Bearing that thought in mind, look up several or all of the following verses and write one to two words describing the actions or attributes of God in each passage.

Genesis 1:1-3	
Exodus 34:6-7	
Deuteronomy 8:5	
Psalm 18:2	
Psalm 33:6	
Psalm 103:13	
Matthew 6:28-30	
Luke 12:32	
John 6:44	
John 10:29	
Romans 1:18	
Romans 5:5	
Romans 8:32	
Romans 11:22	
Galatians 4:4-5	
Ephesians 1:5	
Colossians 1:12	
Colossians 1:13	
Hebrews 10:30	
1 John 4:7-8	
1 John 4:14	

These verses reveal that God is far from a one-dimensional character. He's a real person with a real personality, and His personality consists not only of love but of wrath and justice and a myriad of other things. We can't remake Him to be what we want Him to be. So if this is who He is, then we may be tempted to avoid Him on the bad days when He's leaning into wrath, right? We'll dig into this thought more in the weeks ahead, but as a first step, I want to point out some beautiful hints Scripture gives us about God's personality and character, which are inextricably linked to who He is and what He does.

In the Book of Isaiah, chapters 61 and 62 paint a beautiful picture of the year of the LORD's favor, but chapter 63 turns a corner in describing the day of the LORD's wrath. However, Isaiah gives us some helpful tools for understanding how these things fit together in God's personality. He uses specific terminology to show how God's goodness far outweighs His wrath. For instance, compare the day of His wrath to the year of His favor and redemption (Isa. 61:2; 63:4). That's 365 times more favor than wrath!

One of the verses you looked up in the previous chart was Exodus 34:6-7. Many scholars say this is the most quoted verse within the Bible itself.[6] In the passage, God described Himself to Moses—who He is and what He's like. It paints such a detailed, succinct picture of God—compassionate, gracious, slow to anger, and so forth. Also, God says He keeps faithful love for a thousand generations, but He only punishes to the third or fourth generation.

I wonder if it's possible that the specific order God used to describe Himself carries meaning. Sort of like food labels. When it comes to ingredients, the FDA requires manufacturers to list them in order of predominance.[7] Whatever ingredient is listed first is used in the greatest amount, and the following ingredients are being used in lesser amounts.

He knows we struggle with the idea of wrath. But despite how it makes us bristle, wrath is not the ugly underbelly of God. Even His wrath is praiseworthy. How so? We don't trust people who dismiss evil as "no big deal." Sin has to be punished. When we see wickedness in the world, we want it to be stopped, and we long for justice to be done. We can be comforted to know it's all handled by our loving Father, who is both righteous and good.

Look back at Exodus 34:6-7 and notice how God ordered His characteristics. Summarize the order here.

By the math of Exodus 34 and Isaiah 61–63, it seems God is trying to communicate something to us about His character. Perhaps He's approximately three hundred times more loving. Perhaps He's three hundred times more favor-ful. Probably these are just generalities that don't quite fit on a precise scale. Regardless of how the math works out, it seems God wants to be known for who He really is—a benevolent God full of mercy and grace.

He's a Father worth loving and worshiping. Not only that, He's actually pretty amazing to be around. He's not a drag; He's a delight! He's not looking to smite everyone who defies Him (or else we'd all be annihilated by now). In fact, He's already made a way to completely bridge the gap between His holiness and our sinfulness so we can just enjoy Him! After all, He's where the joy is!

The Weekly Challenge is our practical response to what we've learned in our study and in God's Word this week.

In Romans 5:5, we see the Father's missional heart toward us. Out of His great love, He sent the Son and sends the Spirit. As we seek to extend the Father's love and message to the world around us, we'll aim to be more missional in our lives this week. Ask God to give you at least three ideas for ways you can be "outgoing" in your love and care for others this week. Then aim to do those three things!

> . . . and hope does not put us to shame, because
>
> God's love has been poured into our hearts
>
> through the Holy Spirit who has been given to us.
>
> **ROMANS 5:5**

If weather and health permit, take a thirty-minute prayer walk. If you're unable to go for a walk, try to find a place outside or a quiet spot in your home where you can sit and talk with God. Use the following prompts to guide your prayer time. Silence your phone and set a recurring timer for every ten minutes. Each prompt represents a ten-minute segment of prayer.

 Section A (Minutes 1–10): Thank God for being your Father and adopting you into His family forever. Thank Him for the ways He has Fathered you well and for any new blessings He has brought into your life recently! Thank Him for anything new He has taught you about Himself this week.

 Section B (Minutes 11–20): Ask God to search your heart and reveal any ways you've misunderstood Him as Father. Ask Him to show you if or how you've attached your view of Him to your experience with any earthly fathers or father figures. Repent of (turn from) any ways you've viewed Him wrongly and ask for Him to continue to help you view Him rightly.

 Section C (Minutes 21–30): Talk to God about the healing you need in your relationship with Him as Father or with any earthly fathers or father figures. Ask Him to grant repentance and forgiveness where they may be lacking. Ask Him to bring the healing, peace, restoration, and hope that only He can.

1. OPEN with a time of greeting and prayer.

2. REVIEW your work from this week:
   ☐ Scripture Memory
   ☐ Weekly Challenge
   ☐ Prayer Walk

3. WATCH the Session Three teaching video and use the space below to jot down any notes.

_____

_____

_____

_____

_____

_____

_____

_____

_____

_____

_____

_____

_____

_____

_____

_____

Teaching sessions available for purchase
or rent at *lifeway.com/wherethejoyis*

4. DISCUSS your personal study from last week and today's teaching video using the following questions:

In the past or present, which Person of the Trinity have you felt the most difficulty connecting with? Why?

If you've had a hard time connecting with or trusting God the Father, did anything from this week's study help with that? If so, what was it?

What are some of your favorite attributes of God? Why?

What are some of your least favorite attributes of God? Why?

If we fail or refuse to view God the Father as our Father, how does that impact our ability to love Him and receive love from Him?

In what ways has God the Father shown Himself to be loving toward you? How would you describe the differences between the Immanent Trinity and the Economic Trinity?

Based on what you've learned in this session, why is the Father necessary to our faith?

This week we talked about the importance of reading the storyline of Scripture all the way through, preferably in chronological order, so we can see the story of who God is. Have you ever done that? If so, what did you learn about God through that process?

What was your favorite takeaway from this week's study? How will it impact the way you live this week?

5. CLOSE with prayer.

GOD THE SON

THE WEEK AHEAD

These are the elements of your personal study for the week. Feel free to do them in whatever order works best for your schedule. Check off the items as you move through them.

☐ **DAILY BIBLE READING & PODCAST**

Each day this week you'll read a chapter of Scripture and answer a series of questions to help you reflect on what you read.

☐ Day 1	☐ Day 5
☐ Day 2	☐ Day 6
☐ Day 3	☐ Day 7
☐ Day 4	

☐ **SCRIPTURE MEMORY**

Five days this week you'll work on memorizing 1 John 5:3. Each day you'll find a prompt or easy exercise to help you.

☐ Day 1	☐ Day 4
☐ Day 2	☐ Day 5
☐ Day 3	

☐ **STUDY**

The focus of this session's study is God the Son. You'll learn that He was not born, nor created, but has eternally existed. You'll examine His work in creation and focus on His unique role in redemption as He became God in flesh as Jesus, the Savior of the world.

☐ **WEEKLY CHALLENGE**

The weekly challenge will help you process and respond to what you've studied this week. We encourage you to do this after you've worked through the teaching content.

☐ **PRAYER WALK**

Choose a day this week to prayer walk. We've provided some guidelines to help you structure this time with God.

☐ **GROUP MEETING**

Meet with your group to watch and discuss the teaching video.

DAILY BIBLE READING & PODCAST: **JOHN 8**

🎙️ Read the Daily Bible Reading chapter for the day
or listen to the podcast for the day.

Daily Bible Reading Questions:

Where did you see God show up in the text today?

What did you notice about His character or His attributes?

Did you read anything that pointed to what He loves, what
He hates, what He does, or what motivates His actions? If
so, list what you found below.

To access the daily podcast, visit
lifeway.com/wherethejoyis

DAILY BIBLE READING & PODCAST: **JOHN 9**

🎙 Read the Daily Bible Reading chapter for the day
or listen to the podcast for the day.

Daily Bible Reading Questions:

Where did you see God show up in the text today?

What did you notice about His character or His attributes?

Did you read anything that pointed to what He loves, what He
hates, what He does, or what motivates His actions? If so, list
what you found below.

DAILY BIBLE READING & PODCAST: **JOHN 10**

Read the Daily Bible Reading chapter for the day
or listen to the podcast for the day.

Daily Bible Reading Questions:

Where did you see God show up in the text today?

What did you notice about His character or His attributes?

Did you read anything that pointed to what He loves, what
He hates, what He does, or what motivates His actions? If
so, list what you found below.

SCRIPTURE MEMORY: 1 JOHN 5:3

Today, we start memorizing our next verse. We'll provide different daily prompts on Days Three through Seven each week to help you succeed at this. Since we're memorizing cumulatively—that is, adding to what we learn each week instead of replacing it—we will occasionally recall verses from previous weeks. We gain strength by repetition, so today we'll focus on getting in some reps!

> For this is the love of God, that we keep his commandments. And his commandments are not burdensome.
>
> **1 JOHN 5:3**

Read the verse aloud three times and/or sing along with the verse song if it's helpful.

Write the verse three times in the space provided.

Recite the cumulative verses from all three sessions (1 John 5:1-3) aloud three times.

To sing along with the verse song from the podcast, visit *lifeway.com/wherethejoyis*

4

DAILY BIBLE READING & PODCAST: JOHN 11

Read the Daily Bible Reading chapter for the day
or listen to the podcast for the day.

Daily Bible Reading Questions:

Where did you see God show up in the text today?

What did you notice about His character or His attributes?

Did you read anything that pointed to what He loves, what
He hates, what He does, or what motivates His actions? If
so, list what you found below.

SCRIPTURE MEMORY: 1 JOHN 5:1-3

Everyone who believes that Jesus is the Christ has been born of God, and everyone who loves the Father loves whoever has been born of him. By this we know that we love the children of God, when we love God and obey his commandments. For this is the love of God, that we keep his commandments. And his commandments are not burdensome.

1 JOHN 5:1-3

Read the verses aloud three times and/or sing along with the verse song if it's helpful.

Because it's important for us to not only memorize Scripture but to make sure we comprehend it as well, write our new verse for this week, 1 John 5:3, in your own words.

DAILY BIBLE READING & PODCAST: **JOHN 12**

> Read the Daily Bible Reading chapter for the day
> or listen to the podcast for the day.

Daily Bible Reading Questions:

Where did you see God show up in the text today?

What did you notice about His character or His attributes?

Did you read anything that pointed to what He loves, what
He hates, what He does, or what motivates His actions? If so,
list what you found below.

SCRIPTURE MEMORY: 1 JOHN 5:1-3

Everyone who believes that Jesus is the Christ has been born of God, and everyone who loves the Father loves whoever has been born of him. By this we know that we love the children of God, when we love God and obey his commandments. For this is the love of God, that we keep his commandments. And his commandments are not burdensome.

1 JOHN 5:1-3

Read the verses aloud three times and/or sing along with the verse song if it's helpful.

Today, let's see what kind of progress we're making with our reps. Cover the verses above and then try to write them all from memory. You can glance back if you need to, but be sure to finish each attempt. Keep trying until you're able to write it from start to finish without looking.

DAY

DAILY BIBLE READING & PODCAST: **JOHN 13**

Read the Daily Bible Reading chapter for the day or listen to the podcast for the day.

Daily Bible Reading Questions:

Where did you see God show up in the text today?

What did you notice about His character or His attributes?

Did you read anything that pointed to what He loves, what He hates, what He does, or what motivates His actions? If so, list what you found below.

SCRIPTURE MEMORY: 1 JOHN 5:1-3

Everyone who believes that Jesus is the Christ has been born of God, and everyone who loves the Father loves whoever has been born of him. By this we know that we love the children of God, when we love God and obey his commandments. For this is the love of God, that we keep his commandments. And his commandments are not burdensome.

1 JOHN 5:1-3

Read the verses aloud three times and/or sing along with the verse song if it's helpful.

Try to discover at least three truths in 1 John 5:3 and write them below.

DAY 7

DAILY BIBLE READING & PODCAST: **JOHN 14**

 Read the Daily Bible Reading chapter for the day
or listen to the podcast for the day.

Daily Bible Reading Questions:

Where did you see God show up in the text today?

What did you notice about His character or His attributes?

Did you read anything that pointed to what He loves, what
He hates, what He does, or what motivates His actions? If
so, list what you found below.

SCRIPTURE MEMORY: 1 JOHN 5:1-3

Everyone who believes that Jesus is the Christ has been born of God, and everyone who loves the Father loves whoever has been born of him. By this we know that we love the children of God, when we love God and obey his commandments. For this is the love of God, that we keep his commandments. And his commandments are not burdensome.

1 JOHN 5:1-3

Read the verses aloud three times and/or sing along with the verse song if it's helpful.

If you enjoy creating, try drawing a picture in the space provided of what 1 John 5:3 brings to mind visually for you. If you'd rather not draw a picture, write the verse from memory.

WHO IS THE SON?

The second Person of the Trinity is God the Son. He is the Son because He is eternally begotten of the Father, and His eternality means He isn't younger than the Father. They both exist eternally. God the Son doesn't just reveal Himself to creation—He actually reveals the Father to creation as well, and the Son does it in a way that is unique to Him. While God the Father is spirit, God the Son connected with the physical aspects of creation. We'll study some of the specifics of His relationship with creation throughout this session.

Being the Son makes Him no less God than the Father. Our finite capacity for eternal things makes it difficult for us to grasp how the Father didn't create the Son and that they're both eternal. After all, we've seen family trees and genealogies, and we know how time works. But in order to even scratch the surface of this, we have to detach ourselves from our earthly understanding of time. As the third foundation of the Trinity reminds us, the Father and Son (and Spirit) are co-eternal. But instead of just taking that as fact and nodding our heads, let's dig into Scripture to see what truths helped theologians clarify these foundations over the years.

While the foundations of the Trinity were a regular part of the conversation among the early church, they have flown under the radar so long for us that we barely notice them when we read Scripture. Before we move into the New Testament writings about the Son, let's look at some Old Testament hints about Him. We'll start with a particular passage that reveals who He is. In fact, the first verse in this prophetic psalm is the most frequently quoted Old Testament verse in the New Testament, which tells us the early church regarded it as important and foundational.[1]

> The LORD says to my Lord: "Sit at my right hand, until
>
> I make your enemies your footstool."
>
> **PSALM 110:1**

Read the passage carefully. The verse has two uses of the word _Lord_, but they are written differently. Circle the word LORD where it appears in small caps. Then, underline the word _Lord_ where only the first letter is capitalized.

Using a Hebrew lexicon, look up Psalm 110:1 and write down the Hebrew word translated as _LORD_, along with a brief summary of its meaning or definition.

Then write down the Hebrew word translated as _Lord_, along with a brief summary of its meaning or definition.

Why is it important to note these two unique ways of writing the same word? In the original language, they're two different words with two different functions and meanings. In Hebrew, a language that doesn't use vowels, the name of God was written as "YHWH." Out of reverence, many Jews won't speak it, but others pronounce it as "Yahweh" or "Jehovah." It's most often translated in Scripture as LORD (small caps), and we regard it as God's personal name. His title, on the other hand, is the word _Adonai_ in Hebrew, and it means "Master or Lord." It's most often translated as _Lord_.[2]

Psalm 110:1 may seem peculiar when we first read the English translation, but this information about _LORD, Lord_ helps us clarify the meaning of the verse. And since both words (_LORD, Lord_) can be used to refer to any person of the Trinity, we have some help in understanding what David was communicating here through the Spirit's guidance (Matt. 22:43).

Bear with me because a lot of theology is packed into this tiny verse! King David wrote this psalm thousands of years before God the Son came to live on earth. David said the LORD said to his Lord, "Sit at my right hand." At least a dozen New Testament verses refer to the Son being seated at the right hand of the Father. But those New Testament verses hadn't been written when David wrote this psalm. Still he referred to the Son as his "Lord," the One seated at the right hand of the Father.

In short, this verse is where David overheard God the Father talking to God the Son. David's Lord is God the Son, who had not yet been born into His earthly position but who has always existed nonetheless.

The Son is the only begotten of the Father, beloved of the Father. He is the Word (*Logos*).[3] He is light. He has always been all those things. As we discussed in Session Three, God's "being" and "doing" are interwoven because He always acts out of who He is. As a result, we'll see lots of overlap once again as we aim to dissect the way the Son engages with creation.

Theophanies

Throughout the Old Testament, we have some other bread crumbs that point us toward God the Son. While God the Father is spirit and has no physical form, God the Son, even in the Old Testament, has some unique connections to the physical realm. Because of this, the Son is often attributed with many of the theophanies in Scripture. A theophany is any appearance of God in Scripture that humans could perceive with their senses.

One of the most memorable theophanies in Scripture is when God appeared to Moses at the burning bush (Ex. 3). Some people believe this was God the Father taking on a visible form. Others believe that since humans can't see God and live (Ex. 33:20; John 5:37; John 6:46), these appearances are connected with God the Son instead of the Father.[4]

Some verses associated with theophanies clarify that God is the One appearing (Gen. 22:15-18; Ex. 3:2-4). Others refer to the being who appears as "the angel of the LORD" (Judg. 6:22; Zech. 1:11-13). In these specific instances, three things are worth noting:

1. The Hebrew word for *angel* means "messenger" and doesn't refer exclusively to a type of created being.[5] When angels appear in Scripture, they always appear as or resemble men though they aren't human; they're an entirely different order of created beings, and they are not made in the image of God.

2. Scripture seems to mark out a distinction between "the" angel of the LORD and "an" angel of the LORD. The appearances recognized as theophanies use the terminology *the angel of the LORD*. Whereas most scholars consider appearances describing the spiritual visitor as *an angel of the LORD* to be the created heavenly being.

3. In these theophanies, the being says or does something only God could claim or do.

   Read the following passages. Note whether God is specifically named as the One appearing. If so, note how He is named. If not, what particular claims or actions help identify the being as God? (Hint: Be on the lookout for clues like "LORD" in small caps.)

Genesis 12:7	
Genesis 16:7-13	
Genesis 18:1-2	
Genesis 22:11-18	
Genesis 31:11-13	
Genesis 32:24-30	
Exodus 3:2-6	
Exodus 23:20-21	
Exodus 33:9-11	
Deuteronomy 31:14-15	
Joshua 5:13-15	
Judges 2:1-5	

Judges 6:11-18	
2 Kings 19:33-35	
Job 38:1-3	

None of this means that God the Son was an angel, nor does it mean He was a man—at least not yet. As John Owen described it,

> He was as yet God only; but appeared in the assumed
> shape of a man, to signify what he would be. He did not
> create a human nature, and unite it unto himself for such
> a season; only by his divine power he acted the shape of
> a man composed of what ethereal substance he pleased,
> immediately to be dissolved. So he appeared to Abraham, to
> Jacob, to Moses, to Joshua, and others.[6]

God the Son's role in connecting with humanity has always had a unique physical element to it, which is one reason many theologians believe these appearances could uniquely pertain to God the Son. Another reason is that these unique appearances cease after God the Son comes to earth as the fully-God, fully-man Messiah (Note: *an* angel of the LORD appears after that point, but never *the* angel of the LORD). As with the Trinity, we gain a clearer understanding of these Old Testament appearances in the New Testament. Whether these were preincarnate appearances of God the Son or not, the full revealing of the Messiah and His life, death, and resurrection were still necessary for the completion of God's redemption story.

THE SON IN HIS INCARNATION

Up to this point in the session, I've taken care not to refer to the Son as "Jesus." I've done this for two reasons. First, I wanted to establish that the Son has always existed and that He wasn't merely created when Jesus was born. Second, in eternity past and up until His incarnation, the Son hadn't yet taken on the name Jesus. It's not wrong for us to refer to Him as "Jesus" before His incarnation—and at times it may even be helpful—it's just imprecise. The Son became human when He was conceived in Mary's womb, and He took on the name *Jesus* when He was born in Bethlehem, but He always has been and always will be God the Son.

His eternality is important. In fact, according to Sanders, Jesus' preexistence is "more foundational than his virgin birth."[7] In other words, it's more important where He came from eternally than where He came from temporally. When we say, "Jesus is preexistent," this means He existed before He was human. His eternal nature has always been because He is the uncreated, eternal God. Then, during His time on earth, His eternal, divine nature was united with His human nature. He was both fully God and fully man.

Look up John 1:1-3; Colossians 1:16; and Hebrews 1:2.

According to these verses, what act is attributed to Jesus?

All things were created through God the Son. He built the things the Father spoke into existence with His creation command, showing us once again His unique relationship to the physical realm. It's like God was the architect of Creation, with Jesus bringing those plans into existence.[8] But then Jesus stepped through eternity and into time to live for thirty-three years in the world He built. The only reason the Son is the Son on earth is because He is the Son in eternity. And in order for Him to be God the eternal Son, He must have always existed. To have always existed is to be without a Creator. No one made Jesus; no one made the Son. This is challenging for our brains because we're confined to time, but in the realm of eternity and an eternal triune God, the Son is not younger than the Father. He is, as Scripture and the creeds say, "eternally begotten."[9]

We don't use the word *beget* much in modern language, but the general idea refers to becoming the father of something that is of your own kind. It's unlike creating, which points to something different than yourself. Scripture calls Jesus the "only begotten" Son of the Father

(John 1:14; 3:16, KJV). Since the Father has been fathering eternally, before time, then His Son is eternally begotten and has no point of origin.

The theologians of the early church worked hard to clarify this point, shaping their language precisely in the Nicene Creed: "We believe in one Lord, Jesus Christ, the only Son of God, eternally begotten of the Father, God from God, Light from Light, true God from true God, begotten not made, one in being with the Father."[10] I certainly can't say it better or more clearly than that.

Let's investigate the Son's eternality with our own eyes. Look up the following verses. After each verse, note the phrase(s) used to refer to the lifespan of God the Son.

Isaiah 44:6	
John 8:58	
Revelation 1:8	
Revelation 1:17	
Revelation 22:13	

Why would God the Son come to live on earth as a human? Why would He take on human flesh?

As people who recognize our spiritual poverty, we understand we need someone who is spiritually rich to pay our sin debt. But that only puts us at spiritual "zero"—poor sinners whose debt is paid. God's great love wasn't content to let us stay that way. He didn't want us to be mere strangers who were no longer in debt to Him; He wanted us to be integrated into His family, adopted into His eternal kingdom of righteousness to live with Him forever. In order for that to happen, we don't just need someone to get us to spiritual "zero." We need someone to get us all the way to spiritual righteousness!

In His life and death, Jesus fulfilled both of these roles. By living the perfect, sinless life, He could grant us His righteousness. By dying for our sins, He could pay the debt we owed. We don't just need Christ's death, we need His life too!

Look up the following verses. Put a checkmark by the ones that point to Jesus paying for our sins. Put a star by the ones that point to Jesus granting us His righteousness.

- **Isaiah 53:5**
- **Jeremiah 33:16**
- **Matthew 3:15**
- **Romans 5:6-8**
- **2 Corinthians 5:21**
- **1 Peter 2:24**
- **1 Peter 3:18**

How many of the verses have both a checkmark and a star?

In order for Jesus to both pay for our sins and grant us righteousness, He had to be more than just a good teacher, a wise leader, or a respected prophet. When many people speak of Jesus today, those are the common labels they attribute to Him. People may give a nod to His words about peace and mercy, but they ignore His warnings, His actions, and His claims to be God. In the words of H. Richard Niebuhr, they prefer that the story of the world be one where, "A God without wrath brought men without sin into a kingdom without judgment through the ministrations of a Christ without a cross."[11] They want to escape the responsibility that comes from looking at who Jesus really is because of what it might cost them (John 3:19).

THE SON IN RELATIONSHIP

John 3:16 is a powerful summary of the gospel, and John 15:13 says Jesus' death demonstrated that He has the greatest kind of love for us. But if we disconnect Jesus' love for us from who He says He is in the rest of Scripture, we miss the point entirely. Why would it matter that Jesus loves us or died for us if He's just a good teacher? If that's all He is, nothing shifts in our lives. My first grade teacher loved me, and while that was a real confidence booster that shaped me, it didn't alter my eternity. According to Jesus' claims in John 8:24, we will die in our sins unless we believe He is who He says He is. Since, according to Him, that's so vital, let's look at some of the things He said, did, and claimed to help us form a better understanding of who He is.

Look up the following verses. Beside each verse, write the letter(s) of the action(s) that applies. Some verses may point to multiple scenarios.

A. Jesus did something only God can do.
B. Jesus received worship or didn't rebuke others for claiming He is God.
C. Jesus claimed to be one with the Father.
D. Jesus demonstrated He is distinct from the Father.

- Matthew 14:33
- Matthew 28:9
- Mark 2:5-7
- Mark 10:18
- Luke 22:70
- Luke 24:5-7
- John 5:22
- John 8:48-50
- John 9:38
- John 10:30
- John 11:41-42
- John 11:43-44
- John 14:8-11
- John 14:16
- John 17:1-5
- John 17:21-22
- John 20:28

Jesus talks to the Father, attributes certain things to the Father, claims to be one with the Father, receives worship as God, affirms being the Son of God, and does things only God can do. Taken altogether, these things demonstrate the unique Father-Son relationship of the Trinity. John 1:1 even marks it out for us: Jesus (who is the Word made flesh) both is God and is with God. United with the Father yet distinct from the Father.

This isn't the only aspect of Jesus' personhood that is united yet distinct. This same concept applies to the way His human nature interacts with His divine nature. Theologians call this concept hypostatic union. *Hypostatic* means "personal," and it points to the fact that Jesus is one person, not two people—fully human, fully divine within Himself.[12]

The Council of Chalcedon (AD 451) declared that Jesus is "truly God and truly man" and that His two natures are "without confusion, without change, without division, without separation; the distinction of nature's being in no way annulled by the union."[13] The two natures of Jesus are distinct yet united perfectly. There's a temptation to overlap them, but they can't be blended just as they can't be separated.

Jesus embodied the qualities of both natures. He grew tired, hungry, and thirsty, like every other man (Luke 24:41-42; John 4:6; 19:28). And He raised the dead, could read minds, commanded the weather, and knew the future, like only God can do (Matt. 26:21; Mark 2:8; 4:39; John 11:43). Despite how different His two natures are, they aren't separated; in Jesus, they're united. In fact, they're so tightly bound together that He even makes one nature submissive to the other at times, without losing the attributes of either. For instance, He made His human nature submit to His divine nature when He prayed in the garden of Gethsemane on the night before He died. His human nature wanted to avoid the pain, but His divine nature desired obedience to the Father's plan more than anything else, so His human nature yielded to His divine nature (Matt. 26:39).

The fact that God took on flesh shows us that He is absolutely, unmistakably for us (Rom. 5:8). He released the privileges of His Kingship and came to live as a humble servant among us, pouring Himself into flesh (Phil. 2:6-7). He knows what it feels like to be you. He endured great pains to restore you to the Father because there was no other way for it to happen. Jesus' hypostatic union makes Him perfectly and uniquely suited to be our Savior.

Look up 1 Timothy 2:5 and Hebrews 9:15.

How do these verses refer to the role Jesus plays in our relationship with the Father?

In order to be our Savior, Jesus can't be fifty percent God and fifty percent man; He must be fully and completely one hundred percent both—fully God and fully man. This is why it's impossible for us to find salvation through anyone besides Jesus—He is the only Mediator, the only place where God and man overlap (John 14:6; Acts 4:12). He is the "only begotten Son" (John 3:16, KJV)—the "one of a kind" Son of God— eliminating the possibility of any other mediator.

To summarize R. C. Sproul in *The Work of Christ*, what's remarkable about Jesus isn't that He died on a cross. The Romans crucified thousands of people, perhaps even hundreds of thousands—so that doesn't make Jesus unique. And it wasn't just that He was innocent of what He was accused of; the Romans certainly crucified others who were falsely accused. The uniqueness of Jesus stems solely from His divinity. Being fully God and fully man set Him up to be the bridge between God and mankind. Just as someone who speaks two languages can translate between two people who speak different languages, Jesus is the only means we have for communicating with and being in relationship with the Father.[14]

On the following page, draw two separate circles side by side. Above one write your name. Above the other, write "Jesus."

Inside each circle, write what each person brings to the relationship—either sin or righteousness.

Below each circle, write what we've earned—according to what's inside the circle—either the curse of death or the blessing of life.

Now draw two lines with arrows to indicate the two distinct transfers that have occurred. What does Jesus trade us for our sin? What does Jesus trade us for our death?

Below the drawing, write out the words of 2 Corinthians 5:21.

This illustration should be such a great comfort to us! Knowing that we fall short of God's requirements and have earned the curse of death, we are given an incredible gift that grants Christ's righteousness for free (Rom. 3:21-26; 6:23; 2 Cor. 5:21). Martin Luther reportedly called this the "glorious exchange" where we trade what belongs to us (sin and death) for what belongs to Jesus (righteousness and life).[15] This should set our hearts at ease, knowing that Jesus has accomplished all the Father requires of us.

THE SON'S ACTIONS

In this section, we'll look at a few of the roles specific to the Son. All of Jesus' actions and interactions on earth point us back to the relational beauty of the Trinity. Nothing He does is intended to put the spotlight on Himself.

Look up Philippians 2:5-11 and answer the following questions:

a) Who emptied Jesus?

b) Who humbled Jesus?

c) Who exalted Jesus?

d) At whose name will all people bow?

e) Who will be glorified when all people bow to Jesus?

Jesus emptied and humbled Himself. Some outside force wasn't responsible for it. The Father didn't do it to Him. He did it voluntarily. This helps us see that the Son didn't submit His human will to the Father's plan out of fear of punishment or because He had to; He did it joyfully out of a shared desire. Jesus and the Father wanted the same thing: our rescue!

Look up John 14:31.

Who was Jesus responding to in all of His actions?

Look up John 12:49-50.

Who was Jesus responding to in all of His words?

According to verse 50, what has the Father commanded?

Look up John 10:10.

Why did Jesus come?

Considering your answers to the previous questions, what can you deduce about the Father's intentions toward you?

Everything Jesus says and does aligns perfectly with the Father's will, and everything He says and does is also intended for our flourishing. That means the Father's will for you is that you would flourish! To work out that plan, He sent Jesus to fulfill all that must be fulfilled in order for you to flourish and have eternal, abundant life.

The three divine Persons are inseparable in their unified action toward humanity because each divine Person is engaged in the story and work of redemption. As they work together toward their unified goal, they each have unique roles they've chosen to fulfill. Since their nature is unified, their relationships and roles are what make them distinct. This points back to what we learned about the Economic Trinity in Session Two.

All of the Son's actions are pleasing to the Father. In fact, even before Jesus' ministry began, the Father approved of Him and was pleased with Him (Matt. 3:17). Some of the things we'll look at in the following activity are things He did before His birth. It bears repeating: God the Son has always existed. He was not created.

Look up the following passages and write a few words describing the actions or attributes of God the Son in each passage. (I know there are a lot of verses, but this activity is important, so I encourage you to look up all of them. You may be surprised at what you find in this exercise.)

John 1:3	
John 14:6	
Romans 5:8	
Romans 8:34	
1 Corinthians 15:3-4	
Galatians 3:13	
Ephesians 2:13-18	

1 Timothy 2:5	
Hebrews 1:1-4	
Hebrews 1:10	
Hebrews 4:14	
Hebrews 4:15	
Hebrews 9:28	
1 Peter 2:24	
1 Peter 3:18	
Revelation 5:9	

The Book of Colossians gives us one of the clearest and most concise pictures of who Jesus is and what He has done. Read Colossians 1:9-23 and then write a few words describing the actions or attributes of God the Son in each of the following verses.

Verse 14	
Verse 15	
Verse 16	
Verse 17	
Verse 18	
Verse 19	
Verse 20	
Verses 21-22	

Look back at your responses beside each of the verses in the last two activities. Which of the things Jesus did are things you could do? What does that reveal to you about the work of Jesus and the role He plays in your life?

While Jesus did set an example for us to follow (1 Pet. 2:21), much of what He did is impossible for us. We can't do any of the things you just listed because we aren't divine. I'm not the radiance of the glory of God; you can't build the universe, and neither of us can serve as the mediator between God and man, absorbing His wrath on behalf of all His kids.

But Jesus didn't just come to set a good example for us so that we can get our act together and be acceptable to God. In fact, He came because we can't do those things. We can't live up to His standard. If you have exhausted yourself trying to earn God's favor, you are free to stop striving and rest in the fact that not only did Jesus take on all the Father's wrath toward your sins, but His righteousness has been credited to your account. The list of incredible things Jesus did that you compiled earlier—those are things He has done on our behalf, for our freedom and joy. For our flourishing! He's not just a good teacher. He's so much more than just a moral example for us to follow. He's our complete and utter rescue! He's the deep exhale of complete acceptance and love, despite all our past and future failings (Rom. 8:1).

Jesus fulfills all the Father requires of us (John 19:28-30). And because there is freedom and joy in living the kind of obedient life He lives, Jesus sends His Spirit to live in us, to empower and direct us to that end! He doesn't leave us alone; He sends the Helper (John 14:16), the Spirit. Because God the Son became human and because we are alive in Him, we can participate in and with God! We are united with Him and the Father by the work of the Spirit. We'll read about the Spirit and His role in the next session. He's the One who sustains the Father's work in us, moving us deeper into joy with every step. He's where the joy is!

The Weekly Challenge is our practical response to what we've learned in our study and in God's Word this week.

Read Philippians 2:1-9.

Jesus lived His whole life in humble sacrifice; it wasn't just something He demonstrated on the cross. Write verses 3-5 on a 3x5 card and put it somewhere you'll see often—your mirror, refrigerator, desk, or dashboard (or all of the above!). Whenever you see it, ask God to remind you of the great love He has shown you through Jesus and to prompt you to love others in the same way—out of an overflow of gratitude and joy!

¹So if there is any encouragement in Christ, any comfort from love, any participation in the Spirit, any affection and sympathy, ²complete my joy by being of the same mind, having the same love, being in full accord and of one mind. ³Do nothing from selfish ambition or conceit, but in humility count others more significant than yourselves. ⁴Let each of you look not only to his own interests, but also to the interests of others. ⁵Have this mind among yourselves, which is yours in Christ Jesus, ⁶who, though he was in the form of God, did not count equality with God a thing to be grasped, ⁷but emptied himself, by taking the form of a servant, being born in the likeness of men. ⁸And being found in human form, he humbled himself by becoming obedient to the point of death, even death on a cross. ⁹Therefore God has highly exalted him and bestowed on him the name that is above every name.

PHILIPPIANS 2:1-9

If weather and health permit, take a thirty-minute prayer walk. If you're unable to go for a walk, try to find a place outside or a quiet spot in your home where you can sit and talk with God. Use the following prompts to guide your prayer time. Silence your phone and set a recurring timer for every ten minutes. Each prompt represents a ten-minute segment of prayer.

Section A (Minutes 1–10): Thank Jesus for creating you and the world we live in. Praise Him for living the righteous life you could never live, for granting you His righteousness, and for taking on your sin in His death! Thank Him for anything new He has taught you about Himself this week.

Section B (Minutes 11–20): Ask God to search your heart and reveal any ways you've failed to believe the truth of who Jesus is and what His life, death, and resurrection mean for you. Ask Him to show you if or how you've tried to earn your own righteousness or if you've been dwelling in the shame and condemnation that He says no longer belongs to you. Repent of (turn from) any ways you've viewed Him (and, as a result, yourself) wrongly and ask Him to continue to help you to view Him (and yourself) rightly.

Section C (Minutes 21–30): Talk to the Father about the places you want to see more joy and freedom in your relationship with Him. Ask Him to grow your understanding of Him and give you a deeper desire to keep learning more about Him. Ask Him to give you a deeper understanding of what it means for you to be eternally adopted into His family and called by His name and to know how much He delights in you and approves of you as His child.

1. OPEN with a time of greeting and prayer.

2. REVIEW your work from this week:
   - ☐ Scripture Memory
   - ☐ Weekly Challenge
   - ☐ Prayer Walk

3. WATCH the Session Four teaching video and use the space below to jot down any notes.

_____

_____

_____

_____

_____

_____

_____

_____

_____

_____

_____

_____

_____

_____

_____

_____

_____

_____

_____

Teaching sessions available for purchase or rent at *lifeway.com/wherethejoyis*

4. **DISCUSS your personal study from last week and today's teaching video using the following questions:**

How long has God the Son been the Son? Why is this information vital to our understanding of the Trinity?

Assign someone to read Hebrews 1:1-4 aloud. What does this reveal about the Son's relationship to the Father? How does this help us better understand the Father?

In several parts of this session, we saw how God the Son has a unique relationship with the physical realm. What does it reveal about God that He chose to interact with creation and humanity on such a personal, intimate level?

Why is understanding who Jesus is (i.e. God) necessary in order to see the role His love and His death play in our lives? How does disconnecting Him from His Godhood empty His love and His death of their power?

What do you think flourishing according to God's plan looks like? Does it always amount to easy wins and fulfilled dreams? Have you ever encountered flourishing in the aftermath of trials or as the result of suffering? Explain.

Is it freeing to know that God doesn't expect you to do what Jesus did to earn His affection? Explain.

How can trying to live like Christ be a good thing? How can it be an idolatrous thing? How can you evaluate your motivations to tell the difference?

What was your favorite takeaway from this week's study? How will it impact the way you live this week?

5. **CLOSE with prayer.**

GOD THE
SPIRIT

THE WEEK AHEAD

These are the elements of your personal study for the week. Feel free to do them in whatever order works best for your schedule. Check off the items as you move through them.

☐ **DAILY BIBLE READING & PODCAST**

Each day this week you'll read a chapter of Scripture and answer a series of questions to help you reflect on what you read.

- ☐ Day 1
- ☐ Day 2
- ☐ Day 3
- ☐ Day 4
- ☐ Day 5
- ☐ Day 6
- ☐ Day 7

☐ **SCRIPTURE MEMORY**

Five days this week you'll work on memorizing 1 John 5:4. Each day you'll find a prompt or easy exercise to help you.

- ☐ Day 1
- ☐ Day 2
- ☐ Day 3
- ☐ Day 4
- ☐ Day 5

☐ **STUDY**

In this session's study, you'll dig into perhaps the most misunderstood Person of the Trinity: the Holy Spirit. You'll see how He relates to the Father and the Son and examine His work in individual believers and the church.

☐ **WEEKLY CHALLENGE**

The weekly challenge will help you process and respond to what you've studied this week. We encourage you to do this after you've worked through the teaching content.

☐ **PRAYER WALK**

Choose a day this week to prayer walk. We've provided some guidelines to help you structure this time with God.

☐ **GROUP MEETING**

Meet with your group to watch and discuss the teaching video.

DAILY BIBLE READING & PODCAST: **JOHN 15**

Read the Daily Bible Reading chapter for the day or listen to the podcast for the day. *Note: Choose someone to read the chapter aloud at the meeting or encourage members to read it on their own by the end of the day.*

Daily Bible Reading Questions:

Where did you see God show up in the text today?

What did you notice about His character or His attributes?

Did you read anything that pointed to what He loves, what He hates, what He does, or what motivates His actions? If so, list what you found below.

To access the daily podcast, visit
lifeway.com/wherethejoyis

DAILY BIBLE READING & PODCAST: **JOHN 16**

> 🎙 Read the Daily Bible Reading chapter for the day
> or listen to the podcast for the day.

Daily Bible Reading Questions:

Where did you see God show up in the text today?

What did you notice about His character or His attributes?

Did you read anything that pointed to what He loves, what He hates, what He does, or what motivates His actions? If so, list what you found below.

DAILY BIBLE READING & PODCAST: **JOHN 17**

> Read the Daily Bible Reading chapter for the day
> or listen to the podcast for the day.

Daily Bible Reading Questions:

Where did you see God show up in the text today?

What did you notice about His character or His attributes?

Did you read anything that pointed to what He loves, what
He hates, what He does, or what motivates His actions? If
so, list what you found below.

SCRIPTURE MEMORY: 1 JOHN 5:4

Today, we start memorizing our next verse. We'll provide different daily prompts on Days Three through Seven of each week to help you succeed at this. Since we're memorizing cumulatively—that is, adding to what we learn each week instead of replacing it—we will occasionally recall verses from previous weeks. We gain strength by repetition, so today we'll focus on getting in some reps!

> For everyone who has been born of God overcomes the world. And this is the victory that has overcome the world—our faith.
>
> **1 JOHN 5:4**

Read the verse aloud three times and/or sing along with the verse song if it's helpful.

Write the verse three times in the space provided.

Recite the cumulative verses from all four sessions (1 John 5:1-4) aloud three times.

To sing along with the verse song from the podcast, visit *lifeway.com/wherethejoyis*

DAILY BIBLE READING & PODCAST: **JOHN 18**

Read the Daily Bible Reading chapter for the day or listen to the podcast for the day.

Daily Bible Reading Questions:

Where did you see God show up in the text today?

What did you notice about His character or His attributes?

Did you read anything that pointed to what He loves, what He hates, what He does, or what motivates His actions? If so, list what you found below.

SCRIPTURE MEMORY: 1 JOHN 5:1-4

Everyone who believes that Jesus is the Christ has been born of God, and everyone who loves the Father loves whoever has been born of him. By this we know that we love the children of God, when we love God and obey his commandments. For this is the love of God, that we keep his commandments. And his commandments are not burdensome. For everyone who has been born of God overcomes the world. And this is the victory that has overcome the world—our faith.

1 JOHN 5:1-4

Read the verses aloud three times and/or sing along with the verse song if it's helpful.

Because it's important for us to not only memorize Scripture but to make sure we comprehend it as well, write our new verse for this week, 1 John 5:4, in your own words below.

DAILY BIBLE READING & PODCAST: JOHN 19

Read the Daily Bible Reading chapter for the day or listen to the podcast for the day.

Daily Bible Reading Questions:

Where did you see God show up in the text today?

What did you notice about His character or His attributes?

Did you read anything that pointed to what He loves, what He hates, what He does, or what motivates His actions? If so, list what you found below.

SCRIPTURE MEMORY: 1 JOHN 5:1-4

> Everyone who believes that Jesus is the Christ has been born of God, and everyone who loves the Father loves whoever has been born of him. By this we know that we love the children of God, when we love God and obey his commandments. For this is the love of God, that we keep his commandments. And his commandments are not burdensome. For everyone who has been born of God overcomes the world. And this is the victory that has overcome the world—our faith.
>
> **1 JOHN 5:1-4**

Read the verses aloud three times and/or sing along with the verse song if it's helpful.

Today, let's see what kind of progress we're making with our reps. Cover the verses above and then try to write them all from memory. You can glance back if you need to, but be sure to finish each attempt. Keep trying until you're able to write it from start to finish without looking.

DAY 6

DAILY BIBLE READING & PODCAST: **JOHN 20**

🎙 Read the Daily Bible Reading chapter for the day or listen to the podcast for the day.

Daily Bible Reading Questions:

Where did you see God show up in the text today?

What did you notice about His character or His attributes?

Did you read anything that pointed to what He loves, what He hates, what He does, or what motivates His actions? If so, list what you found below.

SCRIPTURE MEMORY: 1 JOHN 5:1-4

Everyone who believes that Jesus is the Christ has been born of God, and everyone who loves the Father loves whoever has been born of him. By this we know that we love the children of God, when we love God and obey his commandments. For this is the love of God, that we keep his commandments. And his commandments are not burdensome. For everyone who has been born of God overcomes the world. And this is the victory that has overcome the world—our faith.

1 JOHN 5:1-4

Read the verses aloud three times and/or sing along with the verse song if it's helpful.

Try to discover at least three truths in 1 John 5:4 and write them below.

7

DAILY BIBLE READING & PODCAST: **JOHN 21**

Read the Daily Bible Reading chapter for the day or listen to the podcast for the day.

Daily Bible Reading Questions:

Where did you see God show up in the text today?

What did you notice about His character or His attributes?

Did you read anything that pointed to what He loves, what He hates, what He does, or what motivates His actions? If so, list what you found below.

SCRIPTURE MEMORY: 1 JOHN 5:1-4

Everyone who believes that Jesus is the Christ has been born of God, and everyone who loves the Father loves whoever has been born of him. By this we know that we love the children of God, when we love God and obey his commandments. For this is the love of God, that we keep his commandments. And his commandments are not burdensome. For everyone who has been born of God overcomes the world. And this is the victory that has overcome the world—our faith.

1 JOHN 5:1-4

Read the verses aloud three times and/or sing along with the verse song if it's helpful.

If you enjoy creating, try drawing a picture in the space provided of what 1 John 5:4 brings to mind visually for you. If you'd rather not draw a picture, write the verse from memory.

WHO IS THE SPIRIT?

Recall the three foundations of the Trinity and write them below.

I feel like it's a toss-up as to which Person of God is most misunderstood: the Father or the Spirit. While the Father is often misunderstood as being cruel and angry (which we hopefully resolved in Session Three), the Spirit is often misunderstood as being "the mysterious one." He's associated with strange behavior—things we don't see or can't understand—and sometimes rightly so.

But who is He? Is He the Ghost of Jesus left behind on earth after Jesus disappeared? Is He just a force? Does He have a body? Why do we need Him?

God the Spirit is the third Person of the Trinity. But being third doesn't make Him less important or younger than the Father and Son. Like the other two Persons of the Trinity, the Spirit has always existed. He wasn't created after the Son ascended to heaven. While God the Son has a unique connection to the created realm through the incarnation, God the Father is spirit (John 4:24), and God the Spirit is spirit too—and this is important. It impacts the way the Father and Spirit relate to each other and to us as well.

Being God the Spirit makes Him no less God than the Father. He's neither a diluted version of the Father nor the concentration of the Father's power—He's a "he," not an "it." In fact, Matthew 28:19 says He shares a name with the Father and the Son; they could never share their name and oneness with a non-person.

Read John 14:16.

What does each Person of the Trinity do in this verse?

The Son tells the disciples He will pray to the Father and ask Him to send the Spirit, making it clear that Father, Son, and Spirit are all distinct Persons united in their being and shared mission. But how do we know the Spirit isn't merely a force Jesus is using—like His miraculous power?

What did Jesus call the Spirit in John 14:16?

Read Romans 8:26.

What does the Spirit do and how does He do it?

Read Isaiah 63:10 and Ephesians 4:30.

How do we see the Spirit respond to the sin of Israel and to our sin?

These verses reveal that the Spirit is a Person, not a force. Jesus refers to the Spirit as the Comforter (Counselor), not the comfort. The Spirit isn't merely a feeling. In fact, He has feelings. He is deeply, emotionally connected to us. But it would be a mistake to think He is emotional in the same way we are. Our emotions are rooted in our sin nature, so they may be tangled up with sinful motives; but His nature is perfect and so are His emotions. He is grieved by our sin and rebellion, and He groans for us in prayer. We have to be careful not to describe the Spirit using utilitarian language. He's not some impersonal power source we can tap into at our own whims.

What actions did the Spirit take in Acts 8:29; 10:19-20; and 13:2?

The Spirit is a Person who speaks, comforts, guides, takes action, and has a personality. But how do we know that Person is God? In 1 Corinthians 2:10-11, Paul said that no one knows the mind of God except the Spirit of God, who reveals it to us. And if He knows the mind of God, then He knows all things, making Him omniscient. Psalm 139:7-8 reveals He is omnipresent—everywhere at all times. Hebrews 9:14 testifies to His eternality, and Genesis 1:2 says He was there in the beginning, hovering over the waters at creation. He wasn't created. John 15:26 tells us that, contrary to being created by the Father, He proceeds from the Father. In fact, this is one of the chief ways we can describe Him within the Trinity— "the One who proceeds."

Look up the word *proceed* (verb) in a dictionary. What definitions do you find?

As the Spirit proceeds from the Father—and some say He proceeds from the Son as well (John 16:7)—He also declares the truths of Jesus (John 16:13-14). If these connections to the Persons and mission of the Father and Son weren't enough to convince us that the Holy Spirit is God, Scripture makes it clear in the story of Ananias.

Read Acts 5:3-4.

Who did Ananias lie to according to verse 3? And verse 4?

As God, the Spirit shares the same purpose and goal as the Father and Son. They are eternally united. But let's look at His uniqueness more closely. The first time we see God the Spirit in Scripture is in Genesis 1:2. He made several appearances in the Old Testament and during the ministry of Jesus in the Gospels, but the bulk of His activity in Scripture occurs after Jesus ascended to the Father (Acts 1:6-11). The Scriptures referencing Him were written over the course of hundreds of years by dozens of human authors, but they all tell a consistent and unique story about Him, weaving an interesting thread through their descriptions of Him and His work.

Read Genesis 1:2.

What was the Spirit doing in this verse?

Look up the word used for the Spirit's action in a Hebrew lexicon. What other meanings does it have?

Read Matthew 3:16.

What was the Spirit doing in this verse? What is His action compared to?

Read John 3:8.

How did Jesus describe the Spirit's actions?

Read Acts 2:1-4.

How does verse 2 describe the Spirit's actions?

What common thread do you notice in all these verses and descriptions?

From the beginning, the Spirit is connected to, hovering over, and approving of the work of the Father and the Son. He's associated with wind and air. Two of the primary words used to describe Him in both the Old and New Testaments (*ruach*[1], *pneuma*[2]) are closely related to breath and life.

The parallel accounts of the Trinity's activity in both creation and the baptism of Jesus show us their fixed roles. In both events, God the Father was speaking; God the Son was doing, and God the Spirit acted as a hovering seal of approval, enlivening the work. How beautiful! And they use the same pattern in our salvation. God the Father calls us into His family (John 6:37-39); God the Son secures our salvation through His finished work on the cross (John 19:28-30); God the Spirit breathes new life into us and is the seal of our salvation (Eph. 1:13-14).

THE SPIRIT IN RELATIONSHIP
WITH THE TRINITY

The Father, Son, and Spirit work in perfect unity through their specific roles in creation, salvation, and restoration to bring about the fulfillment of God's eternal plan. Throughout Scripture, we see that the Father initiates all divine action, but He doesn't fulfill or sustain it. The Son is the One who accomplished our salvation, but He didn't author it. And the Spirit didn't author it either, but He's the one who applies it. The work of our creation, salvation, and restoration is fully accomplished by the three Persons of the triune God. What a RESCUE they've given us! What a relief to know we're not responsible to save ourselves or to sustain our salvation. When we understand the roles the Trinity plays in our rescue, this incredible truth sets our hearts at ease: He does the doing. What God initiates, He will sustain, and He will fulfill.

James B. Torrance described his salvation like this:

> Firstly, I have been a child of God from all eternity in the heart
> of the Father. Secondly, I became a child of God when Christ
> the Son lived, died and rose again for me long ago. Thirdly,
> I became a child of God when the Holy Spirit—the Spirit of
> adoption—sealed in my faith and experience what had been
> planned from all eternity in the heart of the Father and what
> was completed once and for all in Jesus Christ. There are three
> moments but only one act of salvation, just as we believe there
> are three persons in the Trinity, but only one God.[3]

Even in the Old Testament, the Father spoke of how the Son and the
Spirit are involved in the story of redemption—"I will put my Spirit on him
[Jesus]" (Isa. 42:1, NIV). This was fulfilled at Jesus' baptism, when the Spirit
visibly descended on Jesus in His fluttering, dove-like way. Later, when
Jesus instructed the disciples on baptism, He connected it back to all
three Persons of the Trinity as well. He said to baptize into the name—not
names—of the Father, Son, and Spirit (Matt. 28:19). Jesus underscored
the doctrine of the Trinity in this passage, showing their unity by the use
of the singular name and showing their diversity by the specific references.
It's significant that Jesus' instructions referenced not only Himself, but the
Father and Spirit too. They're all involved, uniquely and unitedly.

**Have you been baptized? If so, could you articulate the doctrine
of the Trinity at the time of your baptism? Would you describe
this as necessary, important, helpful, or unimportant? Why?**

Everything the Spirit does is connected with the Father and the Son. His work echoes outward, pointing to the other Persons of the Trinity—just as they all do for each other in all things. For instance, everything Jesus did during His time on earth was done by the power of the Spirit.

Read the following verses and draw a line matching each reference with the description of how the Spirit empowered Jesus.

Matthew 1:18	The Spirit demonstrates the Father's approval of Jesus.
Matthew 3:16-17	Jesus was conceived by the Holy Spirit.
Matthew 12:28	The Spirit raised Jesus from the dead.
Luke 4:1,14	Jesus testified to the Spirit's anointing on His life and ministry.
Luke 4:16-21	The Spirit guided and sustained Jesus.
Acts 10:37-38	The Spirit empowered Jesus to cast out demons.
Romans 8:11	The Spirit empowered Jesus to die on the cross.
Hebrews 9:14	The Spirit empowered Jesus for miracles and good works.

The Spirit is intimately involved with the work of Jesus, and everything the Spirit does points glory back to the Son. But when Jesus was on earth, since His actions were unprecedented, some people attributed them to demons (Matt. 12:27). In fact, many theologians believe this dismissal—rejection of the Spirit's work through Christ, accusing the Son of God of doing the works of the devil of the Spirit's work—is what Matthew 12:31 refers to as blasphemy of the Holy Spirit, or the "unforgivable/unpardonable sin."[4] Jesus' words and works were all Father-initiated and Spirit-empowered; a rejection of the Spirit is a rejection of the entire Trinity.

The Spirit never points to Himself in His work. He points to Jesus. If you've ever wondered what a Spirit-filled church or person looks like, look for the gospel of Jesus to be proclaimed—that's the pattern of how the Spirit works in Scripture. In Scripture, He never draws attention to Himself for the sake of awe or His own glory; His work is always a means to an end, and that end is the gospel of Jesus. The Spirit reveals Christ. In fact, when Jesus performed Spirit-empowered miracles and people were drawn to Him only for the miraculous performance and not His message, Jesus rebuked them (John 6:26). The Spirit isn't aiming merely to demonstrate God's power, but to use that power to point to God!

Read the following verses. Beside the verse, list each of the things the Spirit does.

John 14:26	
John 15:26	
John 16:14	

Where the message of Jesus is being proclaimed, the Spirit is at work! In fact, one of the ways we most clearly see the Spirit at work is in the very existence of Scripture, which points us to Jesus. According to Jesus, Luke, Paul, and Peter, the Spirit authored Scripture through the hands of men (Matt. 22:43; Acts 1:16; 2 Tim. 3:16-17; 2 Pet. 1:21). He's the One who empowered and guided them as they wrote. Jesus said all Scripture points to Him (John 5:39-46), which is consistent with the rest of the Spirit's work. The Spirit uses His power to communicate the story of God's redemption and love through the work of Christ. This doesn't suggest that the Spirit is some kind of second-tier God. Instead, it reiterates what we've already established: the Persons of the Trinity aren't self-focused; they point to one another and are outgoing in their nature.

THE SPIRIT IN RELATIONSHIP WITH BELIEVERS

The Spirit has been intimately involved with humans ever since His role in creating humanity (Ps. 104:30). When we see Him in the Old Testament, He is most often described as being "on" or "with" a person, and His actions are more transient, moving from person to person to empower them for a specific task. For instance, He came upon Saul to empower him to be king and then left Saul and came upon David when it was time for David to advance to the throne (1 Sam. 10:6; 16:13-14). The Spirit's presence indicated a specific anointing and appointing.

However, in the New Testament, the Father and Son send the Spirit to indwell believers—to seal us and serve as the down payment (guarantee) on our kingdom inheritance. The Spirit is the means by which God is with us always (Matt. 28:20). This is why Jesus said it was to our advantage for Him to leave and send His Spirit instead (John 16:7). The Spirit can be in all believers simultaneously and always—and He is! That is an incredible advantage!

All of the Spirit's actions and interactions on earth point us back to the relational beauty of the Trinity. Nothing He does is intended to put the spotlight on Himself. As we look at His work in our hearts, minds, and lives, we'll see that every aspect of the Christian life is empowered by the Spirit. There's no aspect of our relationship with God that is untouched by the Spirit, and no part of the timeline when He isn't present and active: a) God was already at work in our lives through His Spirit to convict us of sin and draw us to Himself prior to our salvation; b) He is the sign of our adoption and salvation; and c) He remains at work in our lives continually as a result of our salvation.

Prior to our salvation

The Father gives the promise of a new heart and a new spirit (i.e. His Spirit) to His people (Ezek. 36:26-27). The Spirit revealed our need for salvation by convicting us of our sin and our need for a Savior when we were lost (John 16:7-11).

In our salvation

The Spirit makes us new and gives us eternal life (John 3:3-8; Rom. 8:10-11). He washes, regenerates, and renews us (Titus 3:5). He serves as the line of demarcation between the person who knows God and the one who doesn't—without Him, we don't belong to God (Rom. 8:9). He dwells in believers (1 Cor. 6:19). He is the marker of our adoption into God's family (Rom. 8:15), and He makes it possible for us to call God our Father (Gal. 4:6)—without His presence in us through salvation, we would merely be God's creation, not God's children. He is the seal of our salvation, forever marking us as God's possession (Eph. 1:13-14).

And salvation is not just God descending to humanity to rescue us from death and bring us joy in this life. Another beautiful result of our salvation is that, through the power of the Spirit, we're able to ascend with Christ and participate in the Trinity's eternal life and communion (Eph. 2:4-6; 1 John 1:1-4). There is a deep embedding where God unites us with Himself to receive His love eternally.

As a result of our salvation

The Spirit's work in the life of a believer is ongoing, fulfilling God's promise to finish what He started in us (Phil. 1:6). The Spirit, who lives in all followers of Christ, is sanctifying us, maturing us as believers and continually shaping us to look more like Jesus (Rom. 8:29; 2 Cor. 3:18). Without His power in our lives, we would be helpless, hopeless, and joyless!

Romans 14:17 says, "The kingdom of God is not a matter of eating and drinking but of righteousness and peace and joy in the Holy Spirit." Read the following verses and match them with the Spirit's activity in the lives of believers.

John 14:26	Transforms us to be more like Christ
John 16:7	Imparts God's love and hope to us
John 16:8-11	Helps us, guides our prayers, and prays for us
John 16:13	Empowers and equips us to evangelize
Acts 1:8	Our Helper, sent by the Father, teaches us and reminds us of Jesus' words
Acts 8:29	Our Helper, our great advantage in life
Romans 5:3-5	Gives us understanding and wisdom
Romans 8:16	Gives us wisdom, revelation, knowledge, enlightenment, hope, and power
Romans 8:26-27	Guides into all truth
Romans 15:13	Directs our steps
1 Corinthians 2:12-13	Convicts us
1 Corinthians 6:11	Grants us hope
2 Corinthians 3:18	Equips us to walk in holiness, not debauchery
Galatians 5:16-21	Sanctifies and justifies us in Christ
Galatians 5:22-25	Opposes our flesh/natural desires
Ephesians 1:17-20	Enables us to bear His fruit
Ephesians 5:18	Bears witness that we are God's children
Philippians 2:13	Works in us to desire and do God's will

Ths Spirit's activity in our lives is often subtle, specifically when it comes to areas like gaining a new understanding of spiritual truths or being encouraged in our faith. It's tempting to gloss over those things as normal everyday occurrences, but Scripture attributes those actions to the Spirit's loving work in our lives. Likewise, it can be easy to get puffed-up about our obedience, as though we made ourselves live more righteously—but Scripture says the Spirit is the one who transforms us. Our obedience to God is His work in us.

In what ways have you seen your righteousness, peace, and joy increase as a result of the Spirit's work in your life?

Galatians 5:22-23 summarizes the Spirit's activity in the lives of believers by comparing it to fruit, but the word used in this passage is singular, not plural. It is one fruit with nine characteristics: love, joy, peace, patience, kindness, goodness, faithfulness, gentleness, and self-control. Those are the attributes of His fruit—one fruit, nine descriptions—just like you might find multiple ways to describe one apple.

The Spirit's fruit is the opposite of what our nature/flesh desires (Gal. 5:19-21), so while we live on this earth, we're being pulled in two directions. But Paul encouraged us with these words, "Walk by the Spirit, and you will not gratify the desires of the flesh. For the desires of the flesh are against the Spirit, and the desires of the Spirit are against the flesh, for these are opposed to each other, to keep you from doing the things you want to do" (Gal. 5:16-17). Paul told us to follow the Spirit's lead and then lovingly reminded us that we do this out of the joy of our relationship with God, not merely so we can keep God's law: "But if you are led by the Spirit, you are not under the law" (Gal. 5:18). Paul pointed out we're not self-righteous law abiders but Spirit-led fruit producers!

Spirit-fruit may grow slower than you want it to. Sometimes you may notice no progress, and the tree seems barren. In those times, we have to remind our hearts to rest on the finished work of Christ and trust in God's promise to complete what He started in us.

Our position as believers stands in stark contrast to those who don't know Christ. They don't have the Spirit or follow the Spirit, so they lean into the fruit of the flesh ("works of the flesh" in Gal. 5:19-21). Their lifestyle isn't all debauchery—some of it looks more polished and admirable because it takes the shape of power and prestige or even self-focused morality.

In fact, Jesus regularly rebuked the Pharisees, a group of self-righteous leaders in Israel who worked hard to abide by the law. People who are bent on establishing their own righteousness refuse to submit to God instead (Rom. 10:1-4). Jesus said the world (as opposed to God's children) doesn't know the Spirit (John 14:16-17). And those who don't know God don't follow Him; they naturally rebel against Him.

As believers, we're less likely to reject God's work than an unbeliever, but we have another problem to face. If we don't know the details of who the triune God is and how He works in our lives, we're in danger of trying to do His work for Him. We're never told to imitate the Spirit. In fact, we're more frequently called to yield to the Spirit's power than to demonstrate it. We aren't told to be conformed to the Spirit; we're told to be conformed to Christ. The Spirit is the One who enables us to imitate Christ and gives us the desire to do so. His work in our lives is transformative in its very nature. We cannot know Him without being moved toward righteousness, peace, and joy.

God the Spirit is our divine source of power and direction, but if we're captivated by that power simply because we want to use it for our own self-gratification and self-glorification, we not only miss the point, but we reveal our idolatry. The Spirit is for us, but He is God. We are His servants, not vice versa.

THE SPIRIT IN RELATIONSHIP WITH THE CHURCH

One of the most beautiful aspects of the church is the way the Spirit meets the needs of believers. If a church and its members are walking by the Spirit, they'll be leaning into the needs of their people. And because the body of Christ will always have needs and the Spirit knows what they need, He empowers believers in the church with gifts that will help meet those needs. He's so efficient!

> To each is given the manifestation of the Spirit for the
> common good.
> **1 CORINTHIANS 12:7**

According to this verse (which was written to believers), God's Spirit dwells in you and manifests Himself through you as you serve the church. One way to see the Spirit at work in your life is to get involved in the ministries of your church. The gifts He gives for serving the church are wide and varied, but they always point us beyond ourselves to the common good. We don't serve for our own glory or self-esteem.

Read Exodus 31:1-5.

What task did the Spirit empower Bezalel to complete? What was this task for? (Hint: Look back to chapters 25 and 26 if you need help.)

Read Judges 3:9-10.

What tasks did the Spirit empower Othniel for? Who was served or impacted by his giftings?

Read 2 Samuel 23:2.

What task did the Spirit empower David for? Based on the surrounding context, who did this task directly impact? (See verses 1-4.)

Spiritual gifts aren't personality adjacent. They're given by the Spirit and only show up when you have the Spirit. Since He participated in your creation (Job 33:4), He can be credited with your natural giftings too—your talents or abilities, like the way you're athletically inclined, good at math, or are a "born leader." But unlike your natural giftings or inclinations, your spiritual gift may be something you aren't naturally inclined toward. Both types of gifting are God-given and God-driven and are intended to serve others and point glory back to God.

For instance, when God called Moses to be a leader and a prophet in Exodus 4:10-17, Moses protested because he said he was not a gifted speaker. God reassured Moses, reminding him that He would give him all the necessary words. But God also generously provided him with a ministry partner who was naturally gifted at speaking, his brother Aaron. Even though Moses and Aaron existed before the indwelling of the Spirit, God has always been working in His people to fulfill His plan. God uses both our spiritual gifts and our natural gifts to accomplish His purposes. God knows what His people need, and He knows what our leaders need, and either through natural giftings or spiritual giftings, He meets those needs!

Scripture addresses and lists spiritual gifts multiple times: Romans 12:6-8; 1 Corinthians 12; Ephesians 4:11-16; and 1 Peter 4:10-11. What's interesting is that these lists include some repeat roles, but they don't fully overlap, which seems to indicate none of the lists is exhaustive. Since the gifts are different in every place Scripture mentions them, it seems to me that these lists are meant to adapt. More gifts will continue to be added as the needs of the church shift and change because God will continue to equip His people with the spiritual gifts required to meet those needs.

That's one reason why I believe your spiritual gifts may change over the course of your life. There's a good chance your church may need different things at different times, and God will equip specific members with what they need in order to meet the needs of other members. This humbles us and blesses us all at once—it reminds us that we never stop needing each other!

This session may make you curious about your Spirit-given gifts. In my experience, the best and most helpful way to determine what spiritual gifts you have is to see how the church is being built up by your presence there. If you don't know, ask someone at your church! If he/she doesn't know, this may be a great time to look into volunteering or serving at your church. First Corinthians 12:11 says, "All these are empowered by one and the same Spirit, who apportions to each one individually as he wills." The word *wills* suggests this is a volitional act on His part. He is intentional about how He is using you to serve His kingdom! You and your role are not an accident or an oversight!

What spiritual gifts do you believe you have? Why?

How are you currently serving the church?

Do you have natural gifts that you're using to serve the church as well? If so, what are they?

In addition to His work in the believers within the church, the Spirit equips and guides the church by setting apart elders and ministers to lead it (Acts 13:2; 20:28). Ultimately, through all His acts within individual believers and the church at large, the Spirit drives us toward deeper joy. Acts 13:52 says, "The disciples were filled with joy and with the Holy Spirit." All of His giftings and comfort, all of His truth and help, all of His reminders of our eternally secure relationship—He's the One who makes all those things possible for us. He fills us with joy because He's where the joy is!

How would you summarize who God the Spirit is?

The Weekly Challenge is our practical response to what we've learned in our study and in God's Word this week.

Look at your answer to the first question on page 143 in this week's study. Without sharing your answer, ask two people at your church what they think your spiritual gifts are. You might be surprised or encouraged by their answers. If you/they are stumped, use this Weekly Challenge as an opportunity to find out what volunteer positions are open at your church. Find out what the needs are and how God might be calling and equipping you to meet them. (And remember, the opportunities may not necessarily correspond to your natural giftings.)

If weather and health permit, take a thirty-minute prayer walk. If you're unable to go for a walk, try to find a place outside or a quiet spot in your home where you can sit and talk with God. Use the following prompts to guide your prayer time. Silence your phone and set a recurring timer for every ten minutes. Each prompt represents a ten-minute segment of prayer.

 Section A (Minutes 1–10): Thank the Spirit for breathing new life into you and being the sign and seal of your adoption into God's family! Praise Him for the way He comforts you with reminders of your identity in Christ, the way He bears His fruit in your life, and the help He offers you in each moment. Thank Him for anything new He has taught you about Himself this week.

 Section B (Minutes 11–20): Ask God to search your heart and reveal ways you've misunderstood who He is as God the Spirit. Ask Him to point out how you've tried to walk in your own strength instead of asking for His help to obey. Ask Him to reveal the ways you may have tried to abuse His power or gifts for personal gain, empowerment, or self-esteem. Repent of (turn from) the sins He reveals and ask Him to help you view Him rightly.

 Section C (Minutes 21–30): Ask God to help you identify, use, and develop the spiritual gift(s) He's given you. And if there are ways you long to serve the body of Christ (the church), ask the Spirit to give you the spiritual gifts to meet those needs. Ask Him to grow your understanding of Him and to give you a deeper desire to keep learning more about Him. Ask Him to bear more fruit in your life and to guide you into all truth, reminding you of the words of Christ. Ask Him to remind you to ask for His help when you need it, knowing He is already groaning for you in prayer.

GROUP MEETING

1. OPEN with a time of greeting and prayer.

2. REVIEW your work from this week:
   □ Scripture Memory
   □ Weekly Challenge
   □ Prayer Walk

3. WATCH the Session Five teaching video and use the space below to jot down any notes.

_____

_____

_____

_____

_____

_____

_____

_____

_____

_____

_____

_____

_____

_____

Teaching sessions available for purchase or rent at *lifeway.com/wherethejoyis*

4. DISCUSS your personal study from last week and today's teaching video using the following questions:

What would be different about our relationship with the Spirit if He were merely a force, a power, an "it," instead of a "He"?

Which of the Spirit's actions have you seen Him demonstrate in your life most recently?

Have you ever been tempted to want more of the Spirit's power for selfish reasons? How can you tell the difference between pure motives and selfish motives?

What do you think your church community would say your spiritual gifts are? How are they served by your presence in the body of Christ?

Which aspects of the Spirit's fruit have been evident in your life recently? When you first read it, was it offensive to you? If so, why?

How can you tell if you're walking in the flesh versus walking in the Spirit? What are some of the internal evidences that reveal your motives?

5. CLOSE with prayer.

PRAYER
&
COMMUNICATION

#HESWHERETHEJOYIS

These are the elements of your personal study for the week. Feel free to do them in whatever order works best for your schedule. Check off the items as you move through them.

☐ **DAILY BIBLE READING & PODCAST**
Each day this week you'll read a chapter of Scripture and answer a series of questions to help you reflect on what you read.

☐ Day 1   ☐ Day 5
☐ Day 2   ☐ Day 6
☐ Day 3   ☐ Day 7
☐ Day 4

☐ **SCRIPTURE MEMORY**
Five days this week you'll work on memorizing 1 John 5:5. Each day you'll find a prompt or easy exercise to help you.

☐ Day 1   ☐ Day 4
☐ Day 2   ☐ Day 5
☐ Day 3

☐ **STUDY**
Thankfully, we have a triune God who is neither distant nor silent. He wants to communicate with us. Your study this session will explore how we're able to have intimate conversation with the God of the universe.

☐ **WEEKLY CHALLENGE**
The weekly challenge will help you process and respond to what you've studied this week. We encourage you to do this after you've worked through the teaching content.

☐ **PRAYER WALK**
Choose a day this week to prayer walk. We've provided some guidelines to help you structure this time with God.

☐ **GROUP MEETING**
Meet with your group to watch and discuss the teaching video.

DAILY BIBLE READING & PODCAST: LUKE 18

Read the Daily Bible Reading chapter for the day
or listen to the podcast for the day.

Daily Bible Reading Questions:

Where did you see God show up in the text today?

What did you notice about His character or His attributes?

Did you read anything that pointed to what He loves, what
He hates, what He does, or what motivates His actions? If
so, list what you found below.

To access the daily podcast, visit
lifeway.com/wherethejoyis

DAY **2**

DAILY BIBLE READING & PODCAST: **PHILIPPIANS 4**

🎙 Read the Daily Bible Reading chapter for the day or listen to the podcast for the day.

Daily Bible Reading Questions:

Where did you see God show up in the text today?

What did you notice about His character or His attributes?

Did you read anything that pointed to what He loves, what He hates, what He does, or what motivates His actions? If so, list what you found below.

DAILY BIBLE READING & PODCAST: **COLOSSIANS 2**

🎙 Read the Daily Bible Reading chapter for the day
or listen to the podcast for the day.

Daily Bible Reading Questions:

Where did you see God show up in the text today?

What did you notice about His character or His attributes?

Did you read anything that pointed to what He loves, what He hates, what He does, or what motivates His actions? If so, list what you found below.

SCRIPTURE MEMORY: 1 JOHN 5:5

Today, we start memorizing our next verse. We'll provide different daily prompts on Days Three through Seven of each week to help you succeed at this. Since we're memorizing cumulatively—that is, adding to what we learn each week instead of replacing it—we will occasionally recall verses from previous weeks. We gain strength by repetition, so today we'll focus on getting in some reps!

> Who is it that overcomes the world except the one who believes that Jesus is the Son of God?
>
> **1 JOHN 5:5**

Read the verse aloud three times and/or sing along with the verse song if it's helpful.

Write the verse three times in the space provided.

Recite the cumulative verses from all five sessions (1 John 5:1-5) aloud three times.

To sing along with the verse song from the podcast, visit *lifeway.com/wherethejoyis*

4

DAY

DAILY BIBLE READING & PODCAST: **COLOSSIANS 3**

🎤 Read the Daily Bible Reading chapter for the day or listen to the podcast for the day.

Daily Bible Reading Questions:

Where did you see God show up in the text today?

What did you notice about His character or His attributes?

Did you read anything that pointed to what He loves, what He hates, what He does, or what motivates His actions? If so, list what you found below.

SCRIPTURE MEMORY: 1 JOHN 5:1-5

Everyone who believes that Jesus is the Christ has been born of God, and everyone who loves the Father loves whoever has been born of him. By this we know that we love the children of God, when we love God and obey his commandments. For this is the love of God, that we keep his commandments. And his commandments are not burdensome. For everyone who has been born of God overcomes the world. And this is the victory that has overcome the world—our faith. Who is it that overcomes the world except the one who believes that Jesus is the Son of God?

1 JOHN 5:1-5

Read the verses aloud three times and/or sing along with the verse song if it's helpful.

It's important for us to not only memorize Scripture but to make sure we comprehend it as well. Below, write our new verse for this week, 1 John 5:5, in your own words.

DAILY BIBLE READING & PODCAST:
1 THESSALONIANS 5

Read the Daily Bible Reading chapter for the day or listen to the podcast for the day.

Daily Bible Reading Questions:

Where did you see God show up in the text today?

What did you notice about His character or His attributes?

Did you read anything that pointed to what He loves, what He hates, what He does, or what motivates His actions? If so, list what you found below.

SCRIPTURE MEMORY: 1 JOHN 5:1-5

Everyone who believes that Jesus is the Christ has been born of God, and everyone who loves the Father loves whoever has been born of him. By this we know that we love the children of God, when we love God and obey his commandments. For this is the love of God, that we keep his commandments. And his commandments are not burdensome. For everyone who has been born of God overcomes the world. And this is the victory that has overcome the world—our faith. Who is it that overcomes the world except the one who believes that Jesus is the Son of God?

1 JOHN 5:1-5

Read the verses aloud three times and/or sing along with the verse song if it's helpful.

Today, let's see what kind of progress we're making with our reps. Cover the verses above and then try to write them all from memory. You can glance back if you need to but be sure to finish each attempt. Keep trying until you're able to write it from start to finish without looking.

6DAY

DAILY BIBLE READING & PODCAST: **JAMES 5**

Read the Daily Bible Reading chapter for the day
or listen to the podcast for the day.

Daily Bible Reading Questions:

Where did you see God show up in the text today?

What did you notice about His character or His attributes?

Did you read anything that pointed to what He loves, what
He hates, what He does, or what motivates His actions?
If so, list what you found below.

SCRIPTURE MEMORY: 1 JOHN 5:1-5

Everyone who believes that Jesus is the Christ has been born of God, and everyone who loves the Father loves whoever has been born of him. By this we know that we love the children of God, when we love God and obey his commandments. For this is the love of God, that we keep his commandments. And his commandments are not burdensome. For everyone who has been born of God overcomes the world. And this is the victory that has overcome the world—our faith. Who is it that overcomes the world except the one who believes that Jesus is the Son of God?

1 JOHN 5:1-5

Read the verses aloud three times and/or sing along with the verse song if it's helpful.

Try to discover at least three truths in 1 John 5:5 and write them below.

DAY 7

DAILY BIBLE READING & PODCAST: 1 JOHN 5

Read the Daily Bible Reading chapter for the day or listen to the podcast for the day.

Daily Bible Reading Questions:

Where did you see God show up in the text today?

What did you notice about His character or His attributes?

Did you read anything that pointed to what He loves, what He hates, what He does, or what motivates His actions? If so, list what you found below.

SCRIPTURE MEMORY: 1 JOHN 5:1-5

Everyone who believes that Jesus is the Christ has been born of God, and everyone who loves the Father loves whoever has been born of him. By this we know that we love the children of God, when we love God and obey his commandments. For this is the love of God, that we keep his commandments. And his commandments are not burdensome. For everyone who has been born of God overcomes the world. And this is the victory that has overcome the world—our faith. Who is it that overcomes the world except the one who believes that Jesus is the Son of God?

1 JOHN 5:1-5

Read the verses aloud three times and/or sing along with the verse song if it's helpful.

If you enjoy creating, try drawing a picture in the space provided of what 1 John 5:5 brings to mind visually for you. If you'd rather not draw a picture, write the verse from memory.

COMMUNICATION BASICS

> The only person who dares wake up a king at 3:00 AM
> for a glass of water is a child. We have that kind of
> access.[1]
> **TIM KELLER**

People have written many books on prayer, but our focus here will be less on learning how to pray and more on understanding how our view of the Trinity informs and directs our prayers. The way we communicate with the triune God is fully informed by the way we view Him and how much we understand about His actions in our lives. Before we look at how we communicate with Him, let's recap what we've learned about the Trinity so far. It's foundational for every interaction with Him.

Recall the three foundations of the Trinity and write them below.

God the Father, Son, and Spirit are all intimately involved in the story of our redemption. In the past three sessions, we've looked at their unique roles as they apply to humanity (the Economic Trinity). It's important for us to remember that God's actions toward us are borne out of who He is (the Immanent Trinity). He isn't triune because He behaves in these ways; His triune nature precedes and informs all His triune actions.

Here's a brief overview, summarized from Ephesians 1:3-14.

The Father: Our creation, salvation, and restoration originated with the Father. He chose us before the foundation of the world and planned to adopt us as His children (Eph. 1:3-6). His plan was accomplished and applied through the other Persons of the Trinity.

The Son: He accomplished the work of our creation, salvation, and redemption. The Son is the means by which the Father does His saving work in our lives—including our forgiveness, reconciliation, justification, sanctification, and glorification (Eph. 1:7-12).

The Spirit: The Father's salvation (accomplished through the Son) is communicated to us by His Holy Spirit. God gives us His Spirit to dwell in us, making us new, granting us faith, changing us from the inside out, and continuing in us the sanctifying work of conforming us to the image of Christ. The Spirit establishes and confirms that we are God's children, and He serves as a guarantee of our salvation (Eph. 1:13-14).

> Some people look for security in a subjective experience of the Spirit; others in the objective work of Christ. But Christian assurance encompasses both for it has a threefold basis in trinitarian grace. It is rooted in the electing love of the Father, the finished work of the Son, and the present witness of the Spirit.[2]
>
> **TIM CHESTER**

In approximately three to ten words each, summarize the roles each Person of the Trinity played in your creation, salvation, and restoration.

Father:

Son:

Spirit:

In short: the Father authored our salvation; the Son accomplished it, and the Spirit applied it. Knowing that all of this goodness originated with the Father's plan (Jas. 1:17) should endear our hearts to Him. It should serve as a reminder that we are welcomed at His throne and His table (Heb. 4:16). Scripture repeatedly reveals that the Father loves to hear from His children, and He wants us to talk to Him all the time. Not only that, He also delights to give good gifts to His children (Matt. 7:11; Luke 12:32).

Because all three Persons of the Trinity are involved in our creation, salvation, and redemption, it should be no surprise that all three Persons are involved in our prayer life too. In Scripture, the normative way to pray is to the Father, through the Son, by the Spirit. We'll cover that in greater depth later in this chapter, but before we look at how we communicate with God, let's look at how God communicates with us.

HOW GOD COMMUNICATES WITH US

Look up the following verses: John 6:44; John 6:65; 1 John 4:19; Revelation 3:20.

According to these verses, who started the conversation between us and God?

How does it feel to be pursued by God? Is it comforting? Scary? Heartwarming? Threatening? Why?

As the Father is the initiator of all good things, He also is the One who initiates communication with us, His people. He longs to be united with us, but our sin nature means we're separated from Him, which inhibits our communication. But praise God—He had a plan for this all along! Not only did Jesus bridge the gap by granting us His righteousness and making a way for us to approach the Father, but the Spirit came to dwell in us as well, giving us access to a constant flow of communication with God. Just as the Father, Son, and Spirit work together for our creation, salvation, and redemption, they also work together toward our conversation. The Father takes action through the Son by the Spirit, and that's the shape of our communication with Him as well.

Look up Philippians 2:5 in a few different Bible translations (biblehub.com offers this for free).

What is the instruction given to us? Based on what you know about the Trinity, how would this be possible for us? Who would accomplish it and how?

Jesus promised us that the Spirit would remind us of His words (John 14:26). God communicates with us via His Spirit, who equips us with the mental and spiritual truth that Jesus taught and lived and is. As the Spirit works in us, He equips us to think like Jesus thought and live out of the same truth. He can, quite literally, change our minds. This is beautiful, paradigm-shifting news for you if you've ever felt drawn to something you knew wouldn't benefit you or if you've lacked a love for the things of God. If you, like Paul, have ever felt trapped by your own heart and sin patterns (Rom. 7:13-25), the Spirit gives you hope for better things—the mind of Christ! He communicates the truth to us in the midst of sin's lies!

In addition to speaking truth to us through Scripture and the Spirit, God helps us in other ways.

Read Hebrews 7:25.

Who is the active agent in this verse? List all the things He is doing on your behalf.

Read Romans 8:34.

What is Jesus doing for you? When is He doing it?

Read Romans 8:26-27.

Who is the active agent in these verses? List all the things He is doing on your behalf.

Scripture tells us that both the Son and the Spirit are praying for you. Not only is this a great comfort, but it's a great promise. God didn't save you then abandon you. He is praying for you. According to 1 Corinthians 2:10-11, the Spirit knows the thoughts of the Father, and, in fact, they share a will and nature, so the Spirit is praying things for you that align with the Father's heart and His plan for you. God has promised to always answer yes to prayers that align with His will (1 John 5:14-15), which means these prayers prayed by God to God are ones He will answer with a yes. None of them are fruitless or frivolous. They all point toward your redemption and your ultimate joy!

Read 1 Corinthians 2:10-11.

List all the things these verses reveal about the Spirit and His actions.

Not only does the Spirit pray to the Father on our behalf, He also teaches us how to pray to the Father. If you've ever felt like you're not good at praying or you feel awkward praying in front of others, take heart! The Spirit is willing and able to teach you how to pray. We can learn from Him through the examples of prayer He has shown us in Scripture, including when Jesus taught His disciples how to pray. As the Spirit teaches us, He also serves as a conduit for our communication with the Father. He never angles for our attention; He's always pointing us back to the Father through the work of the Son.

HOW WE COMMUNICATE WITH GOD

Prayer is irksome. An excuse to omit it is never unwelcome.

. . . We are reluctant to begin. We are delighted to finish.[3]

C. S. LEWIS

How do you most often begin your prayers? Why?

How do you most often end your prayers? Why?

Many of us learned to pray by listening to others pray. We may have learned patterns that feel formal or "right," but some of them likely hold no meaning to us. If we've never taken the time to understand prayer by studying the examples in Scripture, it may feel like a meaningless exercise, like divine small talk. But it is so much more! Since prayer is communicating with the living God, let's begin with what we know about Him. Let's not just operate out of habits that aren't informed by our relationship with Him. Now that we know more about Him, we can talk to Him in ways that are more honest, accurate, and personal—and when we bend our prayer life around the truth of who He is, our relationship with God will begin to take on richer textures and deeper joys!

> The theological mind exists to throw logs into the furnace of our affections for Christ.[4]
>
> **JOHN PIPER**

Why do you pray? List as many reasons as you can think of. Circle the reason that shows up most frequently in your prayer life.

Most of the prayers we see throughout Scripture aren't aimed at personal success; they're oriented toward a personal knowing of God—but it's not just informational knowledge; it's relational knowledge. For those who truly seek God in prayer, the relationship is not only central; it is supreme. It is the most important goal, and that perspective is what drives the conversation.

Jesus demonstrated this for us when He prayed. To paraphrase Fred Sanders, in the New Testament, we get to eavesdrop on Jesus' prayers to the Father. We get to hear the things He told the disciples about the Spirit. We hear the Father's words to the Son. Lots of these things happen in public settings, and Jesus even prayed aloud, letting others hear and see the intimacy of His relationship with the Father. We get a glimpse into the unity of the triune.[5] Gerald Bray said, "Christians have been admitted to the inner life of God."[6]

Look up the following verses: Luke 10:21; Luke 22:17-19; John 11:38-42.

What do Jesus' prayers in these three passages have in common?

Look up 1 Thessalonians 5:16-18.

What is God's will for you?

One of the things we learn from eavesdropping on Jesus' prayers is that He thanks and praises the Father. He acknowledges the Father's role in things both big and small—from providing the food to His attention to Jesus' prayers to the way He works in the hearts of humanity. When we see how Jesus talks to the Father, we get a glimpse into the Father as our ultimate Provider, loving Father, and sovereign King. In addition to that, Jesus is an example of how our hearts should arc toward God with gratitude and praise in all things, which is one of the things Scripture clearly marks out as God's will for us in 1 Thessalonians 5:16-18.

Read the Lord's Prayer in Matthew 6:9-13.

To whom does Jesus instruct us to pray?

The structure of trinitarian prayer mirrors both the way God communicates with us and imparts salvation to us. The Father communicates with us through the connection established by the work of His Son, sustained by the power of the Spirit. And our responsive prayer to Him flows through that same flow of communication: we pray by the Spirit, through the Son, to the Father.

We pray to the Father. In the Lord's Prayer, Jesus instructed His followers to pray to the Father. That doesn't mean we can't or shouldn't pray to the Son or Spirit, but it shows us that the normative way of praying is directed to the Father. Jesus tells us that the Father is a willing listener who is eager to give good gifts to His children.

> The God who had the idea of you is interested in you . . . He
> is a God far more willing to answer and hear our prayers
> than we are to offer them.[7]
> **SAM ALLBERRY**

We pray to the Father through the Son. Jesus is the One who bridges the gap between us and the Father—that's what it means to pray "in His name." It's not a magical add-on that ensures we get what we ask for; it's the key for entry into the conversation. He is always the mediator for our conversations with the Father. Praying in His name is a reminder that we don't come on our own merit or performance but on His merit and performance. It's an invitation to always show up in prayer because we can be certain the Father's desire to hear us is unchanging, unyielding. Because Jesus bridged the gap, we can approach the throne of grace with confidence, knowing God will hear us and will show us mercy and help us when we need it (Heb. 4:16). No matter what sin you've committed, no matter how much you've failed, you're welcome at His throne. Then, on the other hand, when you feel like you've nailed it as a Christian and pride creeps in, coming to the Father through the Son and in His name humbles us. We can't come to the Father in our own names. As Allberry said, "We come to the Father not by the sweat of our brow but by the blood of his Son."[8]

We pray to the Father through the Son, by the Spirit. Allberry added, "No Christian prayer happens apart from the work of the Spirit. We may not be mindful of that as we pray, but it is true."[9] According to Romans 8, the effect of the Spirit in our lives is that we're not only adopted into God's family, we also rightly recognize ourselves as God's children—we gain a sense of our new, true identity. As we pray, we're deepening and strengthening our relationship with God because we're engaging with Him more and more. The Spirit comes alongside us and helps us know how to pray.

Since He is with us, indwelling us as we pray, we never pray alone. And none of our prayers are wasted, even if God's answer to our prayer is no.

Prayer is a form of worship, and "worship is . . . our participation through the Spirit in the Son's communion with the Father, in his vicarious life of worship and intercession."[10] Prayer reminds us of how deeply embedded we are in the life and community of the triune God and arcs our hearts toward Him as we engage with Him in conversation.

Look up Psalm 141:2.

What is prayer compared to in this verse?

Look up Revelation 5:8.

What is the setting of this scene? What is being presented before the Lamb?

Our prayers are compared to incense, a tool the ancient Jews used as a part of their worship process in the temple. Not only are our prayers received as worship, but they're presented in treasured vessels, golden bowls. It's astonishing that God regards the prayers of His people so highly—to count them as worship, to cherish and guard them. Your prayers are valuable to God! He loves to communicate with you!

When we pray, we're participating in the trinitarian life, engaging with all three Persons of the Trinity. If your prayers are self-seeking and you only talk to God in order to ask Him for what you want, consider this an invitation to talk to God about deeper things. The point of prayer is not to get what we want; the point of prayer is to get God. The more intimate a relationship is, the less we're able to function autonomously—we consider the other person, we look to honor him/her in our words and actions. And so it is with God. Through intimacy with Him, we connect with the source of all good things (John 15:5-11), and intimacy comes from the private conversation of prayer. How comforting it is to know that God wants prayer that is rooted in intimacy, not showiness. He doesn't care how many syllables your words have or how many words you use—He's after your heart!

THE MYSTERIES OF PRAYER

Prayer remains mysterious to us even as we engage in it. Sometimes we let that mystery intimidate us and keep us from communicating with the Father. But as we're learning more about trinitarian prayer, this is your opportunity to lean in—don't let what you don't yet know stop you. In fact, the impulse to pray comes to us from God Himself; He is relational, and He communicates within Himself and with us!

> We may have built walls against prayer, against the presence
> of God, because of things he has not given us, things we
> thought we deserved. We may be blind to the blessings He
> has given us and think only of those things He has withheld.
> We may be refusing to enter into any mentality that accepts
> loss and defeat as trials given for our growth and perfection.
> We may be refusing to pray because we don't intend for
> God to have it His way.[11]
> **EMILIE GRIFFIN**

Look up John 16:23-23 and James 4:2.

What is the encouragement in John 16 and the implication in James 4?

Our God is eager to give! It's His nature. And He can only give what is good and best. Even in the difficult things that come our way, the eternal reality is that our Father can be trusted. And our trust in Him can coexist with any pain, sadness, or anger we may feel in our current circumstances. He aches with us. Knowing that it's not in our good Father's nature to give bad gifts, we can pray and ask while we ache and wait.

Based on your current understanding of Scripture, why would God tell His children no or wait when they ask for something? Can you think of any verses that speak to this?

Is it hard for you to accept God's no or wait in response to your prayer? Why or why not?

Every time we come before God, humble ourselves in His presence, and ask Him to meet our needs, it shows we acknowledge Him as the source of all things. When we pray, we declare our faith in His character and His ways. But we must be careful to remember that this is our faith in Him, not faith in our faith or faith in our actions. I can't believe something hard enough to make it happen, and I can't force His hand through my obedience. He's not indebted to me, and He doesn't owe me a yes. It's easy to assume that if we want something and it's not sinful, then it is good, and we deserve it. But God's plan involves giving us more than just what we perceive as good—He's determined to give us what is best in the scope of eternity, and that's something we don't have the wisdom to perceive!

Read Ephesians 3:20-21.

What do these verses say God will do?

This is why we want God to say no to us at times. We can't even begin to conceive the things He has in store for us! Our plans are far too small and temporary. His plans to bless us exceed our ability to imagine. Surely you've begged God for something that you later thanked Him for saying no to. I know I have! His no is always for the greatest good, and because we aren't eternal like He is, we don't have eyes to see what He sees.

Even Jesus, being fully God and fully man, had human longings that the Father said no to. In Luke 22:42, on the night before Jesus died, He prayed, "Father, if you are willing, remove this cup from me. Nevertheless, not my will, but yours, be done." And in knowing what was the eternal plan, Jesus' human nature submitted to His divine nature, yielding to the Father's will. Our humanity must also submit to His divinity and yield to the Father's will.

How do we make sure we're yielded to God in prayer and that we're not trying to take over for Him? We need the Spirit's help. Paul told us that we should pray "at all times in the Spirit" (Eph. 6:18). What does that mean? When quoting Myers' Commentary, John Piper described it like this: Praying in the Spirit is praying in such a way so "that the Holy Spirit is the *moving* and *guiding* power" of the prayer.[12] In other words, we are actively engaging with Him as we pray, decidedly yielding to His guidance, not autonomously praying out of our own desires and experiences.

Draw near to Him in prayer today. He will meet you there—in your longings, confusion, sin, and gratitude—and He will be the loving Father you need in all those categories. He's where the joy is!

> God will either give us what we ask for in prayer or give us what
> we would have asked for if we knew everything he knows.[13]
>
> **TIM KELLER**

The Weekly Challenge is our practical response to what we've learned in our study and in God's Word this week.

We've learned a lot about prayer in this week's study. Let's put our new knowledge to work using these three Ps: Practice, Posture, and Pattern.

Practice: Every day this week, aim to carve out five minutes for the practice of private prayer. It may be helpful to set a reminder alarm on your phone for the same time each day so you don't forget.

Posture: During your prayer time, consider positioning yourself in one of the postures of prayer we see demonstrated in Scripture: kneeling, lying facedown, lifting arms upward, bowing at the waist, and so forth. These positions are more than just a way to show our reverence to God; they also help us stay focused so our minds don't wander from the conversation (which can be challenging with all we have going on in our minds each day!).

Pattern: As you're praying, be mindful of what you've learned about the normative pattern of prayer in Scripture: praying to the Father, through the Son, by the Spirit.

Pray expectantly and be on the lookout for the ways this practice enriches your relationship with the triune God this week!

If weather and health permit, take a thirty-minute prayer walk. If you're unable to go for a walk, try to find a place outside or a quiet spot in your home where you can sit and talk with God. Use the following prompts to guide your prayer time. Silence your phone and set a recurring timer for every ten minutes. Each prompt represents a ten-minute segment of prayer.

 Section A (Minutes 1–10): Thank the Father for inviting you into conversation, for caring about all the details of your life, for making a way for you to communicate with Him and equipping you with the faith to pray. Tell God about all the ways you have a new delight in Him, in who He is, and what He does. Thank Him for anything new He has taught you about Himself this week.

 Section B (Minutes 11–20): Ask God to search your heart and reveal any ways you've taken communication with Him for granted—whether it's praying, reading His Word, or leaning in to the promptings of His Spirit. Repent of (turn from) any ways you've viewed Him wrongly or failed to listen to Him.

 Section C (Minutes 21–30): Ask God to equip you with truth and speak to you, to give you wisdom and understanding. Ask Him to grant your heart the right desires so that you might pray for things He delights to say yes to. Ask Him to give you a deeper longing for His Word and a greater sensitivity to His Spirit so that your time in prayer and in Scripture might bear more fruit than ever before.

GROUP MEETING

1. OPEN with a time of greeting and prayer.

2. REVIEW your work from this week:
   - ☐ Scripture Memory
   - ☐ Weekly Challenge
   - ☐ Prayer Walk

3. WATCH the Session Six teaching video and use the space below to jot down any notes.

_____

_____

_____

_____

_____

_____

_____

_____

_____

_____

_____

_____

_____

_____

_____

_____

_____

Teaching sessions available for purchase
or rent at *lifeway.com/wherethejoyis*

4. **DISCUSS your personal study from last week and today's teaching video using the following questions:**

Have you ever thought about who you direct your prayers to? Who are you most inclined to address? Why?

Describe a time when you changed your mind about something—either because you gained more information or because you felt God moving your heart in a different direction.

Why do you pray? Does it change your motivation to know that God treasures your prayers? If so, how?

If you had to rank the order of your most common prayers, how would you order these categories: praise/thanks, requests for guidance or help, requests for personal desires, confession, praying for others?

Have you ever asked God for something you're now grateful He said no to? How long did it take you to realize His answer was best? What did you learn in the process?

What are some things you're tempted to do in your own wisdom instead of talking to God about first? How has falling into that temptation gotten you in trouble in the past?

Have you ever been afraid to pray? Why? What did you fear would happen? How did God respond to you in your silence?

What was your favorite takeaway from this week's study? How will it impact the way you live this week?

5. **CLOSE with prayer.**

IN HIS IMAGE

These are the elements of your personal study for the week. Feel free to do them in whatever order works best for your schedule. Check off the items as you move through them.

☐ **DAILY BIBLE READING & PODCAST**
Each day this week you'll read a chapter of Scripture and answer a series of questions to help you reflect on what you read.

☐ Day 1   ☐ Day 5

☐ Day 2   ☐ Day 6

☐ Day 3   ☐ Day 7

☐ Day 4

☐ **SCRIPTURE MEMORY**
Five days this week you'll work on memorizing 1 John 5:6. Each day you'll find a prompt or easy exercise to help you.

☐ Day 1   ☐ Day 4

☐ Day 2   ☐ Day 5

☐ Day 3

☐ **STUDY**
We close the study by looking at how God has redeemed us and is constantly at work in conforming us into the image of Christ. We are now imitators of Christ, making God known in the world.

☐ **WEEKLY CHALLENGE**
The weekly challenge will help you process and respond to what you've studied this week. We encourage you to do this after you've worked through the teaching content.

☐ **PRAYER WALK**
Choose a day this week to prayer walk. We've provided some guidelines to help you structure this time with God.

☐ **GROUP MEETING**
Meet with your group to watch and discuss the teaching video.

DAILY BIBLE READING & PODCAST: **PHILIPPIANS 2**

Read the Daily Bible Reading chapter for the day
or listen to the podcast for the day.

Daily Bible Reading Questions:

Where did you see God show up in the text today?

What did you notice about His character or His attributes?

Did you read anything that pointed to what He loves, what
He hates, what He does, or what motivates His actions? If
so, list what you found below.

To access the daily podcast, visit
lifeway.com/wherethejoyis

DAILY BIBLE READING & PODCAST: **EPHESIANS 2**

🎤 Read the Daily Bible Reading chapter for the day
or listen to the podcast for the day.

Daily Bible Reading Questions:

Where did you see God show up in the text today?

What did you notice about His character or His attributes?

Did you read anything that pointed to what He loves, what He
hates, what He does, or what motivates His actions? If so, list
what you found below.

DAILY BIBLE READING & PODCAST: **EPHESIANS 3**

Read the Daily Bible Reading chapter for the day, or listen to the podcast for the day.

Daily Bible Reading Questions:

Where did you see God show up in the text today?

What did you notice about His character or His attributes?

Did you read anything that pointed to what He loves, what He hates, what He does, or what motivates His actions? If so, list what you found below.

SCRIPTURE MEMORY: 1 JOHN 5:6

Today, we start memorizing our next verse. We'll provide different daily prompts on Days Three through Seven of each week to help you succeed at this. Since we're memorizing cumulatively—that is, adding to what we learn each week instead of replacing it—we will occasionally recall verses from previous weeks. We gain strength by repetition, so today we'll focus on getting in some reps!

This is he who came by water and blood—Jesus Christ; not by the water only but by the water and the blood. And the Spirit is the one who testifies, because the Spirit is the truth.

1 JOHN 5:6

Read the verse aloud three times and/or sing along with the verse song if it's helpful.

Write the verse three times in the space provided.

Recite the cumulative verses from all six sessions (1 John 5:1-6) aloud three times.

To sing along with the verse song from the podcast, visit *lifeway.com/wherethejoyis*

4

DAY

DAILY BIBLE READING & PODCAST: **EPHESIANS 4**

Read the Daily Bible Reading chapter for the day or listen to the podcast for the day.

Daily Bible Reading Questions:

Where did you see God show up in the text today?

What did you notice about His character or His attributes?

Did you read anything that pointed to what He loves, what He hates, what He does, or what motivates His actions? If so, list what you found below.

SCRIPTURE MEMORY: 1 JOHN 5:1-6

Everyone who believes that Jesus is the Christ has been born of God, and everyone who loves the Father loves whoever has been born of him. By this we know that we love the children of God, when we love God and obey his commandments. For this is the love of God, that we keep his commandments. And his commandments are not burdensome. For everyone who has been born of God overcomes the world. And this is the victory that has overcome the world—our faith. Who is it that overcomes the world except the one who believes that Jesus is the Son of God? This is he who came by water and blood—Jesus Christ; not by the water only but by the water and the blood. And the Spirit is the one who testifies, because the Spirit is the truth.

1 JOHN 5:1-6

Read the verses aloud three times and/or sing along with the verse song if it's helpful.

Because it's important for us to not only memorize Scripture but to make sure we comprehend it as well, write our new verse for this week, 1 John 5:6, in your own words below.

5

DAY

DAILY BIBLE READING & PODCAST: 1 JOHN 2

Read the Daily Bible Reading chapter for the day or listen to the podcast for the day.

Daily Bible Reading Questions:

Where did you see God show up in the text today?

What did you notice about His character or His attributes?

Did you read anything that pointed to what He loves, what He hates, what He does, or what motivates His actions? If so, list what you found below.

SCRIPTURE MEMORY: 1 JOHN 5:1-6

Everyone who believes that Jesus is the Christ has been born of God, and everyone who loves the Father loves whoever has been born of him. By this we know that we love the children of God, when we love God and obey his commandments. For this is the love of God, that we keep his commandments. And his commandments are not burdensome. For everyone who has been born of God overcomes the world. And this is the victory that has overcome the world—our faith. Who is it that overcomes the world except the one who believes that Jesus is the Son of God? This is he who came by water and blood—Jesus Christ; not by the water only but by the water and the blood. And the Spirit is the one who testifies, because the Spirit is the truth.

1 JOHN 5:1-6

Read the verses aloud three times and/or sing along with the verse song if it's helpful.

Today, let's see what kind of progress you're making with your reps. Cover the verses above and then try to write them from memory. You can glance back at it as needed, but be sure to finish each attempt. Keep trying until you're able to write it from start to finish without looking.

DAY

DAILY BIBLE READING & PODCAST: 1 JOHN 3

Read the Daily Bible Reading chapter for the day
or listen to the podcast for the day.

Daily Bible Reading Questions:

Where did you see God show up in the text today?

What did you notice about His character or His attributes?

Did you read anything that pointed to what He loves, what
He hates, what He does, or what motivates His actions? If
so, list what you found below.

SCRIPTURE MEMORY: 1 JOHN 5:1-6

> Everyone who believes that Jesus is the Christ has been born of God, and everyone who loves the Father loves whoever has been born of him. By this we know that we love the children of God, when we love God and obey his commandments. For this is the love of God, that we keep his commandments. And his commandments are not burdensome. For everyone who has been born of God overcomes the world. And this is the victory that has overcome the world—our faith. Who is it that overcomes the world except the one who believes that Jesus is the Son of God? This is he who came by water and blood— Jesus Christ; not by the water only but by the water and the blood. And the Spirit is the one who testifies, because the Spirit is the truth.
>
> **1 JOHN 5:1-6**

Read the verses aloud three times and/or sing along with the verse song if it's helpful.

Try to discover at least three truths in 1 John 5:6 and write them below.

DAY 7

DAILY BIBLE READING & PODCAST: 1 JOHN 4

Read the Daily Bible Reading chapter for the day or listen to the podcast for the day.

Daily Bible Reading Questions:

Where did you see God show up in the text today?

What did you notice about His character or His attributes?

Did you read anything that pointed to what He loves, what He hates, what He does, or what motivates His actions? If so, list what you found below.

SCRIPTURE MEMORY: 1 JOHN 5:1-6

Everyone who believes that Jesus is the Christ has been born of God, and everyone who loves the Father loves whoever has been born of him. By this we know that we love the children of God, when we love God and obey his commandments. For this is the love of God, that we keep his commandments. And his commandments are not burdensome. For everyone who has been born of God overcomes the world. And this is the victory that has overcome the world—our faith. Who is it that overcomes the world except the one who believes that Jesus is the Son of God? This is he who came by water and blood— Jesus Christ; not by the water only but by the water and the blood. And the Spirit is the one who testifies, because the Spirit is the truth.

1 JOHN 5:1-6

Read the verses aloud three times and/or sing along with the verse song if it's helpful.

If you enjoy creating, draw a picture in the space provided of what verse 6 brings to mind visually for you. If you'd rather not draw a picture, write the verse from memory.

CREATION & RE-CREATION

Recall the three foundations of the Trinity and write them below.

> Then God said, "Let us make man in our image, after our likeness" . . . So God created man in his own image, in the image of God He created him; male and female he created them.
> **GENESIS 1:26-27**

In your own words, recall the ways each of the Persons of the Trinity participated in your natural birth (creation) and write them below.

Read 1 Peter 1:3 in the NASB or ESV Bible.

Who caused us to be born again? How?

In your own words, recall the ways each of the Persons of the Trinity participated in your spiritual birth (re-creation, salvation) and write them below.

The triune God not only worked together in unity and diversity to create us, but all three Persons of the Trinity also worked together in our *re*-creation (Ezek. 36:26-27). The position from which God created the world was one of love and glory. Many theologians believe this is what prompted Him to create the world—to share His infinite happiness and joy with us! What that ultimately means for us is that we will only find true happiness and joy as we connect with His identity and purpose—loving and glorifying God with a love that points us outside ourselves to Him and to others.

In fact, that is precisely how Jesus summarized all of the commands of God: love God, love others (Matt. 22:37-40). It's the very purpose for which we were created. Paul reminded us of this when He called us to "be imitators of God" (Eph. 5:1). If our created purpose is to love and connect with Him, then it stands to reason we would sense a compelling need to live toward that purpose. God generously created that need to point our hearts back to Himself so that we wouldn't be left to wander. Our hearts are prone to seek purpose and fulfillment in a million different temporary things, but He knows He's the true and eternal fulfillment of our needs.

> If God had not a communicative, spreading goodness, he would never have created the world. The Father, Son, and Holy Ghost were happy in themselves, and enjoyed one another before the world was. Apart from the fact that God delights to communicate and spread his goodness, there had never been a creation or redemption.[1]
>
> **RICHARD SIBBES**

CONFORMED TO CHRIST (WHO MADE THE FATHER KNOWN)

Adam and Eve were created in God's image, but did that all change when they sinned? Was His image in humanity ruined or lost? Not according to Scripture. Thank God, His image in us extends beyond the garden of Eden. It wasn't erased by the fall. Let's look at some of the places we see this in Scripture.

Based on Genesis 9:6, why is murder a sin? According to James 3:9, why is cursing others a sin?

To summarize Donald Macleod in *Shared Life*, we retain the image of God for as long as we live, despite our sin.[2] That goes for even those who don't know God. Being made in God's image means we all have equal worth even in our diversity, and it means we're built for community and fellowship, just like the triune God. But in addition to being created in God's image, Scripture says we are to be conformed to Christ's image.

Read Romans 8:29 and rewrite it in your own words. It may help to break the verse down phrase by phrase.

What does it mean that Jesus is "the firstborn among many brothers"?

Jesus, in His position of prominence and perfection, is the reason we can be adopted into God's family. He was the first and only One to perfectly reveal God to humanity in the flesh, but now we all follow His lead, albeit in our humanity and imperfection.

Here's what that looks like when we zoom out on the overall storyline of God's interactions with us:

A. God the Father sent God the Son to earth to show humanity what He is like. B. God the Son willingly took on the bounds of the earthly realm when He entered into it. He demonstrated the Father's heart to us, showing His compassion, His affection for sinners, His pursuit of our hearts and our joy— not just our adherence to His laws. C. After fulfilling the Father's demands on our behalf, the incarnate Son returned to the Father in heaven but sent His Spirit to dwell in all His followers so that we might be the demonstration of the Father's heart within the earthly realm.

Through the work of God the Spirit in us, we are one of the primary ways the world sees what God is like. While Scripture and creation reveal Him as well, many people may never read Scripture or acknowledge God as the Creator of the universe, so we have a unique role in revealing Him to those around us. We were created in the flesh, and we are recreated in the Spirit—raised from the dead to "walk in newness of life" (Rom. 6:4-5). This is what new life looks like, to share in His death and resurrection! We love the idea of sharing in His resurrection, but the preceding verse (Rom. 6:3) and the following verses talk about sharing in His death.

Circle the words *die, died, dead,* or *death* every time they appear in the passage below.

> For one who has died has been set free from sin. Now if we have died with Christ, we believe that we will also live with him. We know that Christ, being raised from the dead, will never die again; death no longer has dominion over him. For the death he died he died to sin, once for all, but the life he lives he lives to God. So you also must consider yourselves dead to sin and alive to God in Christ Jesus.
>
> **ROMANS 6:7-11**

Draw a square around the words *live, life,* and *alive* every time they appear in the passage above.

Scripture gives us snapshots of many ways we're being conformed to the image of Christ through the process of our life, death, and resurrection. Look up the verses below and match each verse with its description.

John 15:8	Sent like Him
John 20:21-22	Suffer like Him
Romans 8:17	Identify with Him
1 Corinthians 15:49	Resurrected like Him
Philippians 3:20-21	Transformed like Him
Hebrews 13:12-13	Glorified with Him

How can these things be possible for us, mere humans? And how will we endure the more trying aspects of these things? Scripture also has good news—shocking news—for us along these lines. Not only does God the Spirit live in us, but all three Persons of the eternal triune God live in us!

Look up the following verses and write each reference under the column it corresponds to. Some verses may fit under multiple columns. (Note: most references to "God" in these particular passages are often considered to be references to the Father.)

- John 14:17
- John 14:18-20
- John 14:23
- John 15:4-5
- Romans 8:11
- 1 Corinthians 6:19
- Galatians 2:20
- Ephesians 3:17
- 1 John 4:12
- 1 John 4:16

God the Father lives in us.	God the Son lives in us.	God the Spirit lives in us.

This reaffirms one of the most comforting, beautiful truths of Scripture: God is not tentative about us. He is not hedging His bets—one foot in relationship, the other out the door. He has set His heart fully on us; He is completely bought in and has already paid the full price. We are eternally guarded by God's presence in our lives. As such, this reinforces our eternal security. Having His nature and His presence marks our adoption into His family.

> Christ is God's Son eternally: we become God's sons and daughters only when we receive Jesus (John 1:12). He is God's Son by nature; we become God's children by grace (1 John 3:1). But the relationship itself is essentially the same. We are heirs of God and *co-heirs* with Christ (Rom. 8:17). We have exactly the same inheritance. According to John 17:26, we are loved with the same love.[3]
>
> **DONALD MACLEOD**

What a stunning truth! Not only are we conformed to the image of Christ, but we are loved with the same love as Christ, indwelled by the triune God, and empowered to demonstrate the goodness of God to the world around us!

IMITATORS OF CHRIST (TO MAKE THE FATHER KNOWN)

One of the supernatural byproducts of being redeemed by God and conformed to the image of Christ is that we will begin to act like Him. Our internal transformation is revealed. This is what Jesus was referring to when He said, "By this my Father is glorified, that you bear much fruit and so prove to be my disciples" (John 15:8).

Just as Jesus walked in obedience to the Father (John 15:10) through this continual abiding, God's abiding in us means we're able to walk in a unique kind of power over sin and the flesh (Rom. 8:37; Phil. 4:13). This power calls us to be mindful of our eternal purposes, to walk by the Spirit and not by the flesh, since both the power and glory of the eternal God dwells in us. To summarize Macleod, God is always in our space, which means every sin we commit is committed "under his very nose."[4] And yet when we do sin, He does not leave us or forsake us. In fact, we would have no power over sin if He did leave us. He knows He is our only hope for change, because He is the One who equips us to imitate Christ.

Look up Romans 2:4.

What leads us to repentance?

Read 2 Timothy 2:25.

Where does repentance come from?

Look up Ezekiel 36:26-27.

How/why do we obey God?

We've seen how the Persons of the Trinity are uniquely and unitedly involved in our creation and salvation. In the same way, they continue to participate in our sanctification—working together toward the goal of conforming us to the image of Christ.

When you think of Jesus, what descriptive words come to mind?

Which of the descriptive words you just listed do you long to see Him demonstrate through you more? Circle those words and then write out a short prayer asking Him to make you more like Him.

Michael Reeves said, "Christianity is not primarily about lifestyle change; it is about knowing God."[5] He also said, "What we love and enjoy is foundationally important. It is far more significant than our outward behaviour, for it is our desires that *drive* our behaviour. We do what we want."[6]

Centuries earlier, the French philosopher Blaise Pascal said it this way:

> **All men seek happiness. This is without exception. Whatever different means they employ, they all tend to this end. The cause of some going to war, and of others avoiding it, is the same desire in both, attended with different views. The will never takes the least step but to this object. This is the motive of every action of every man, even of those who hang themselves.[7]**

We do what we want. We all seek our own happiness. In light of this, it's important to ask ourselves: *what do we want; what do we love; and where do we believe happiness is found?*

Ephesians 5:1-2 calls us to be imitators of Christ: "Therefore be imitators of God, as beloved children. And walk in love, as Christ loved us and gave himself up for us, a fragrant offering and sacrifice to God."

Why would we want to imitate Him? Or anyone? We imitate what we find beautiful and desirable. When you see someone with shoes you like, you probably wish you had them too. Maybe you even want to go buy those shoes for yourself. And even beyond that, when you find something you love, you want others to love it too. We want the world to find what we've found, so we talk about it and spread the word. We put bumper stickers on our cars, wear logos on our T-shirts, and generally become walking commercials for things we want to be associated with. We are always pointing to something beyond ourselves, but nothing we point to is eternal unless it is God Himself. Everything else will fall apart or fade out of fashion.

As we aim to imitate Christ, what specifically should we imitate? I've heard comedians talk about what it's like to do an impression of someone else—they say you first have to pick up on the things that stand out about her most before you move to the subtle nuances. You emphasize her drawl or her famous hand gestures or a phrase she repeats often.

Which of Jesus' character traits seems to define Him most? (You can look back to your list of descriptive words for help.)

When you think about Jesus, perhaps you think about His resurrection or His miracles—His actions. But if you zoom in on the character and personality that lies underneath all His actions, one thing stands out to me as His most noteworthy attribute: *Jesus is known for His love.* Love has always been true of the Persons of the Trinity throughout all eternity. And in fact, it's what He calls us to imitate about Him: "love one another as I have loved you" (John 15:12).

Take heart—you aren't called to imitate His ability to walk on water or turn it into wine. You're called to love. But sometimes that seems even harder, doesn't it? Somehow, bending the laws of nature feels less challenging than speaking loving words to the family member who voices his/her disapproval of all your decisions. Or showing love to the stranger online whose political opinions grate against the core of your personal beliefs. When faced with the call to love those people, you feel more equipped to raise Lazarus from the dead!

Loving others is hard work, but loving only yourself is a godless, joyless endeavor. As Tim Keller said in his book *The Reason for God*, "Nothing makes us more miserable than self-absorption, the endless, unsmiling concentration on our needs, wants, treatment, ego, and record."[8] The good news is: if you struggle to love people well, you don't have to do it on your own. You don't have to muster up love or fake it. In fact, you can't. So how do you do it?

Here's what it looks like to imitate God and His love. First, remember that God has generously, abundantly poured out His love to you. Because of that, you can dial into the love you've received from Him, you can remember His patience and compassion toward you. Second, as you recall His love toward you, you can ask Him to ignite that same love in your own heart as you engage with Him to respond to those who are difficult for you to love. They aren't difficult for Him to love. And He actually lives inside you and promises to guide you! Don't be surprised if you feel the Spirit prompting you with an idea: *Here's how you do it.* It's kind of like having the golf pro stand with you and put his hands over your hands and do the swing for you. He does the doing!

As we imitate God, it's important to remember that we don't imitate Him in order to impress Him. He knows what He's like, and He knows what we're like (Ps. 103:14). And He knows the only way we can imitate Him is through His work in us. He gets the glory, and we get the joy. Ultimately, we imitate Him because He's the path to joy—for us and for others!

THE BODY OF CHRIST

The Persons of the Trinity all work together to accomplish the redemptive plan for humanity, which serves as a great reminder for us that we're designed to do our best work in community. As much as God is at work in you, you alone aren't capable of demonstrating His love in all the ways necessary to reveal Him to a world in need. First of all, you have to sleep at some point. Second, you can only be in one place at a time. And third, you're limited in your finances, resources, and skills. Fortunately, God has already pieced all these things together. In Session Five ("God the Spirit"), we talked about the various spiritual gifts God has given us and how they serve to benefit the church. We don't all have all the gifts, which means we need each other! God lovingly planted us in a family of Christ-followers, the church, and as we work together in unity with our unique skills and passions, we demonstrate His love to a watching world!

Look up Romans 12:4-5; 1 Corinthians 12:27; and Colossians 1:18.

What theme(s) do you notice in these verses?

The church is the body of Christ because we are united with the body of Christ. And Jesus longed for and prayed for us to be united with each other in the same kind of unity He shares with us and with the Father.

> **The verses below are part of a prayer Jesus prayed to the Father, referencing all who will believe in Him across the whole course of history, including you! Circle each time Jesus used the words *one* and *in*.**

> I do not ask for these only, but also for those who will believe in me through their word, that they may all be one, just as you, Father, are in me, and I in you, that they also may be in us, so that the world may believe that you have sent me. The glory that you have given me I have given to them, that they may be one even as we are one, I in them and you in me, that they may become perfectly one, so that the world may know that you sent me and loved them even as you loved me.
>
> **JOHN 17:20-23**

Our unity with each other stems from the fact that we all have the same relationship to God. Every other Christian is our brother or sister in Christ, chosen and adopted by Him into His family. And we all are indwelled by Him. In fact, we are not just individually the dwelling place of God, but the church itself is the dwelling place of God. Ephesians 2:18-22 describes us as a building God is establishing, with Jesus as its cornerstone, "in whom the whole structure, being joined together, grows into a holy temple in the Lord. In him you also are being built together into a dwelling place for God by the Spirit" (vv. 21-22).

As eternal family, we're not only inextricably joined with Him, but with each other too. And to be fair, "joined" is probably too small a word to capture the dynamics and dimensions of this relationship—we are fused, grafted into it.

Read 1 John 4:7-21.

What command serves as bookends for this passage about God's love for us?

God's love for us not only reveals how we should love, but it also compels us to love. Just as God is outgoing in His love, we should be too! We are deeply involved with Him and with each other on every level of kingdom life, though it's often challenging to remember this and live it out. The picture Scripture paints is one where Christ-followers of various tribal, political, and socioeconomic backgrounds live together with Christ as their focus. Among Jesus' disciples, He had the wealthy tax collectors and the poor fisherman; He had those who worked for Rome and those who wanted to overthrow Rome; He welcomed those who were considered filthy and godless—pagans, prostitutes, and lepers.

What a beautiful demonstration not only of His love and unity, but of His diversity! Not only did Jesus live in this way, but His followers did too. The early church, which was made up primarily of circumcised Jews, began to see an influx of Gentile followers after the coming of the Holy Spirit, but they didn't demand circumcision of them (Acts 15:1-21). Their primary concern was that their shared belief in Jesus not be disrupted by division. But this definitely wasn't a seamless process. Change can be difficult for any of us, especially where religious beliefs are concerned, and it often results in conflict as people adjust. That's what happened with the early church. They had to get through some bumpy times to throw open the doors of the gospel. Even the leaders struggled at times. In fact, Paul had to call out Peter when he caved to peer pressure and disregarded the Gentile believers, choosing to eat only with the Jewish believers. Paul rebuked him for showing partiality, which is divisive (Gal. 2:11-14).

Jesus spent more time identifying Himself with His church as a whole than with any one individual. For instance, prior to his conversion to Christianity, the apostle Paul was an outspoken persecutor of Christians. When the voice of the resurrected, ascended Christ spoke from heaven and confronted Paul about His actions, He asked, "why are you persecuting me?" (Acts 9:4). Jesus was already back in heaven, but He was identifying Himself with the persecution of the church. Additionally, Scripture calls Jesus "the head of the body" (Col. 1:18), and the head certainly knows and experiences all that the body endures.

The New Testament repeatedly affirms the connection between the unity of the church and the triune life of God. Just as God's unity and diversity is revealed in His triune nature, we participate in the triune life through the Son, being united in Him in our diversity. Donald Macleod said, "We must be careful not to set this unity and this diversity over against each other. The church is not one *despite* its diversity but *because* of its diversity."[9] This is harmony not homogeny. Every person playing the same instrument with the same note does not make a symphony. But different instruments hitting different notes to the same rhythm and key of the same song? That's beautiful! The Economic Trinity has demonstrated this for us, working out a unified will and purpose through distinct roles to accomplish it.

As the people who are made in His image, conformed to His image, and called to imitate Him, we should expect that others will be drawn to Him through our lives and witness! The very love that rescued us is pursuing others who don't yet know Him, and He's using us as His ambassadors in that process.

When others see our relationship with God, our hope is that they'll want to have that relationship too!

Jesus commanded His disciples to make disciples. The word *disciple* means "learner."[10] He wanted the learners to learn, then teach. He told them to baptize the new disciples, but He didn't just say to baptize them in His own name—He said to baptize them in the name of the Father, and of the Son, and of the Holy Spirit. We are baptized into Christ—buried and raised with Him—and this is how we participate in the communion of the Trinity. Our verbal confession and action of being baptized are important, but we need to understand that baptism is fundamentally about who we are. It's about our union with the triune God.

Since many professing believers know very little about the three Persons of the Trinity, we have failed terribly at obeying Jesus' command in our lives and in our churches. It's vital that the doctrine of the Trinity not be glossed over, but be widely taught and understood among professing Christians. That's one of the reasons it's so important that you've finished this study!

Considering your newfound knowledge of the Trinity and the things about the triune God you've been reminded of in this study, spend some time meditating on the following questions and write what God brings to mind:

What does it look like to reveal God to the world around us?

What does it mean to be His image-bearers?

How do the persons of the Trinity help us live out His unified will and purpose in the world?

How can our hearts be at peace in the midst of the chaos around us?

What is the ultimate purpose for the family of God?

Our new, richer understanding of who God is will begin to inform everything about the way we make peace with our past, live in the present, look to the future, and interact with others around us. Knowing Him better changes the way we know ourselves. Knowing Him better changes the way we love others. Now that we see Him more clearly, we can confidently say: He's where the joy is!

The Weekly Challenge is our practical response to what we've learned in our study and in God's Word this week.

As you aim to imitate God and His love this week, recall the love He has generously, abundantly poured out to you. Remember His patience and compassion toward you. Ask Him to show you someone who needs to feel His love this week and how you can be a vessel that pours His love out to others. He may bring to mind someone who is dear to you whom you're excited to serve. Or He may bring to mind someone you find difficult to love. If it's the latter, remember that he/she isn't difficult for Him to love. As you aim to imitate His love toward him/her, remember He lives inside you and promises to guide you! He does the doing!

If weather and health permit, take a thirty-minute prayer walk. If you're unable to go for a walk, try to find a place outside or a quiet spot in your home where you can sit and talk with God. Use the following prompts to guide your prayer time. Silence your phone and set a recurring timer for every ten minutes. Each prompt represents a ten-minute segment of prayer.

Section A (Minutes 1–10): Thank the Father for His great love for you. Praise Him for the fact that He has set His heart fully on you and isn't scared away by your sin but that He instead stays close, showing kindness to prompt repentance in you. Thank Him for being a God worth imitating and a God worth demonstrating to the world around you!

Section B (Minutes 11–20): Ask God to search your heart and reveal any ways you've tried to imitate Him for the wrong reasons—to impress Him or others or to earn love. Ask God to reveal any ways your heart doesn't mirror His. Repent of (turn from) any ways you've viewed Him wrongly and ask Him to continue to help you to view Him rightly.

Section C (Minutes 21–30): Ask Him to direct your heart to want the right things, to seek happiness at its true source: HIM. Ask Him to help you love others, especially those in the church, and to remind you that He has also set His heart of love on them. Ask Him to equip you with all you need to love others well by first receiving His love and then extending it to others.

GROUP MEETING

1. OPEN with a time of greeting and prayer.

2. REVIEW your work from this week:
   - ☐ Scripture Memory
   - ☐ Weekly Challenge
   - ☐ Prayer Walk

3. WATCH the Session Seven teaching video and use the space below to jot down any notes.

_____

_____

_____

_____

_____

_____

_____

_____

_____

_____

_____

_____

_____

_____

_____

_____

Teaching sessions available for purchase
or rent at *lifeway.com/wherethejoyis*

4. **DISCUSS your personal study from last week and today's teaching video using the following questions:**

What have you tried to find fulfillment in? Success? Beauty? Debt freedom? Marriage? Children? Influence? In what ways have these things failed to fulfill you? How does life reveal those things are merely temporary?

What is the point of us being conformed to the image of Christ?

Do you ever feel the impulse to run from God when you sin? Where does this impulse come from?

If all Christians are supposed to be conformed to the image of Christ, how will the church maintain the diversity that God intentionally created? How will we avoid becoming homogenized?

In what ways have members of the body of Christ demonstrated His love to you?

Unity is our best reality, but it's not always possible or right. What are some things that should not divide a church body? What are some things that should divide a church body?

What was your favorite takeaway from this week's study? How will it impact the way you live this week?

What is your favorite takeaway from this study overall? How has it informed your relationship with God and the joy you have in knowing Him?

5. **CLOSE with prayer.**

LEADER HELPS

Hey leaders! Thanks for taking on the blessing and responsibility of leading your group through the *He's Where the Joy Is* study. I know the task might seem a little daunting, especially since it's a study on the Trinity, but you can do this. Keep in mind, you're not being asked to teach the study but to facilitate it. That means you don't have to know everything or have all the answers! Make use of all the resources we've provided for you and allow the Holy Spirit to guide you. You're going to do great!

This Leader Helps section is an abbreviated version of what I talk about on the Leader Training video, so I strongly encourage you to watch that first as you prepare to lead. This section can serve as a short checklist.

First, let's talk about your GROUP MEETINGS.

General Thoughts

1. Start and end on time. This will be a blessing to everyone because they've all carved out time in their busy lives to make this happen, so it's helpful to keep with the schedule.

2. Meet in an inviting space. It's a bonus if that space includes a place where everyone can sit around a table.

3. Encourage everyone to silence their phones and put them away.

4. Do your best to create a distraction-free zone for the meeting.

Meeting Schedule

Now let's talk about some of the components of each session's group meeting. What will you do? In what order? How do you transition? First, we'll cover what to do in your Launch Meeting (Group Meeting One), and then we'll list what we suggest for Group Meetings Two through Seven.

Group Meeting One/Launch Meeting

The Launch Meeting is the first time your group will meet. Here's a suggested agenda:

1. Welcome group members and use the following questions to break the ice and get your group talking:

    • Why are you interested in doing a study about the Trinity?

    • How would you define the Trinity?

    • Which Person of the Trinity are you most excited to learn more about? Why?

    • Based on your current understanding, how would you explain the roles the Persons of the Trinity have played in the story of your salvation? What might be some Bible verses that speak to these roles?

2. Distribute the *He's Where the Joy Is* Bible study books and encourage your members to take a quick look through them. Direct them to the first Launch Meeting page (p. 11).

3. Show the Session One video and invite members to jot down any notes or questions during the teaching.

4. After the video, allow participants to voice any questions or comments about what they heard. Spend as much time as needed helping group members get familiar with the layout of the sessions.

5. As you close your time, briefly walk participants through Session Two, pointing out the different components of the study and emphasizing that this is their starting spot for the next week.

6. Close the Launch Meeting in prayer.

Group Meetings Two through Seven/Weekly Meetings

This is our suggested meeting agenda. Feel free to arrange the following components to serve your group and time constraints.

1. Open in PRAYER. You can vary how this takes place.

2. Offer your group the opportunity to practice their MEMORY VERSES. If you have a smaller group, consider going around the circle and encouraging every person to say the verse out loud. If your group is larger, ask your members to pair off or say the verse to the person sitting beside them.

3. Check in with your group about what they learned in the WEEKLY CHALLENGE. This gives you a chance to see how the study is bearing fruit in the lives of your group members. It also serves as a great segue into the teaching video!

4. Watch the TEACHING VIDEO. Prior to the session, make sure your TV or computer works, including the speakers. Set a good example by giving your full attention to the video each week and taking notes.

5. Following the video, lead the GROUP DISCUSSION. You might want to include some introductory questions, such as:

   - What was your biggest takeaway from the personal study this week?
   - What questions about the Trinity arose from your study this week?

We've also included several questions and discussion prompts on the Group Meeting pages for each session. Feel free to use these to help foster discussion. You can add or delete questions according to the makeup of your group, time frame, and the leading of the Holy Spirit.

6. Close with a PRAYER EXPERIENCE. Feel free to vary this each week. Options include large group prayer led by one person or a select few, praying in pairs or small groups, popcorn prayer, written prayers, and so forth.

GENERAL LEADER INSTRUCTIONS

1. Be PREPARED. Make sure to watch the teaching video and do all the personal work through the week. You want to set the example for your group members. Plus, this will help you be ready to lead the group

discussion. Also, be spiritually prepared. Spend time with the Lord each day. Teach from the overflow of what He's pouring into you.

2. Be SENSITIVE. Let the Holy Spirit guide you as you prepare and lead your group. Be sensitive to the needs of your members and be willing to adjust your plan to address pain points in what they're learning and applying.

3. Be ENCOURAGING. Understand this study could be a spiritual and mental stretch for some of your group. Cheer them on as they work, not just in the group meeting but throughout the week with a note, email, call, or text. And pray for them!

YOU ARE DOING A GREAT WORK for the kingdom! Remember, you aren't responsible for the response of your members. You're only responsible for the way you lead. So be faithful and obedient. And know that there will be fruit for your labors. In John 15:8,11, Jesus said, "By this my Father is glorified, that you bear much fruit and so prove to be my disciples. . . . These things I have spoken to you, that my joy may be in you, and that your joy may be full." I want you all to bear the mark of God's blessing and to feel the joy He has for you in this study and in this role of leadership. I can't WAIT to dig into this study with you and learn more about God together! Lean in, my friends! Because He's where the joy is!

GLOSSARY

CONSUBSTANTIAL: regarded as the same in substance or essence[1]

DOCTRINE: Christian teaching on a specific subject[2]

ECONOMIC TRINITY: the external work of the Trinity (as it relates to creation and humanity)[3]

GLORIFY: to show as worthy, to praise, to appreciate, to serve, to please[4]

HYPOSTATIC UNION: the doctrine of the two natures, divine and human, in the single person of Jesus Christ[5]

IMMANENT TRINITY: the internal life of the triune God[6]

MONOTHEISM: belief in the one true God who is the sovereign Creator[7]

POLYTHEISM: belief in many gods[8]

PROGRESSIVE REVELATION: God didn't reveal His whole plan for His people at one time. He worked through His process via different means, patiently giving us more information piece by piece, at just the right time.[9]

THEOLOGY: a set of beliefs about God[10]

We all have beliefs about God, so you're already a theologian! Our goal is to be good theologians who believe true things about God that are consistent with Scripture. That means we'll always be adding to (and sometimes adjusting) what we know about God as we search Scripture and learn more of what it teaches us about God.

THEOPHANY: any appearance of God in Scripture that humans can perceive with their senses; predominantly used to describe visible revealings[11]

HERESIES

A heresy is any belief or teaching that denies one or more of the foundational truths about God. These are some of the heresies denying Scripture's teachings about the Father, Son, and/or Spirit.

Arianism: a heresy denying that Jesus is truly God; denied Christ's full divinity, stating that Christ was a created being who was superior to human beings but inferior to God[1]

Docetism: a heresy that says Jesus wasn't actually human but only appeared to be human[2]

Gnosticism: a heresy that says the body and all physical things are corrupt so Jesus could not really be human[3]

Henotheism: a heresy that says the god(s) in charge vary at different locations around the world or for different people groups[4]

Modalism: a heresy that says God is one person who appears to us in three different forms rather than three distinct persons ("Jesus Only," "Jesus Name Movement," and "Oneness Pentecostalism" are associated with this.)[5]

Monarchianism: a heresy that stresses the unity of God so heavily that it discounts God's plurality as three distinct Persons[6]

Monophysitism: a heresy that says Jesus' divinity fully absorbed His humanity, so that, in the end, He was only divine and not human[7]

Nestorianism: a heresy that says Jesus was a human person who was joined to the divine Son of God[8]

Polytheism: a heresy that says there are many gods[9]

Subordinationism: a heresy that says Jesus is not created, but He is still inferior to the Father, and thus not equal to the Father in being and attributes[10]

Tritheism: a heresy that says the Trinity consists of three separate Gods[11]

(Many groups who reject the Trinity often falsely accuse or misunderstand those who believe in the Trinity as holding this position.)

Unitarianism: a heresy that says God is only one Person instead of three Persons[12]

ATHANASIAN CREED

We worship one God in trinity and the trinity in unity,
neither blending their persons
nor dividing their essence.
For the person of the Father is a distinct person,
the person of the Son is another,
and that of the Holy Spirit still another.
But the divinity of the Father, Son, and Holy Spirit is one,
their glory equal, their majesty coeternal.

What quality the Father has, the Son has, and the Holy Spirit has.
The Father is uncreated,
the Son is uncreated,
the Holy Spirit is uncreated.

The Father is immeasurable,
the Son is immeasurable,
the Holy Spirit is immeasurable.

The Father is eternal,
the Son is eternal,
the Holy Spirit is eternal.

And yet there are not three eternal beings;
there is but one eternal being.
So too there are not three uncreated or
immeasurable beings;
there is but one uncreated and immeasurable being.

Similarly, the Father is almighty,
the Son is almighty,
the Holy Spirit is almighty.
Yet there are not three almighty beings;
there is but one almighty being.

Thus the Father is God,
the Son is God,
the Holy Spirit is God.

Yet there are not three gods;
there is but one God.

Thus the Father is Lord,
the Son is Lord,
the Holy Spirit is Lord.
Yet there are not three lords;
there is but one Lord.

Just as Christian truth compels us
to confess each person individually
as both God and Lord,
so catholic religion forbids us
to say that there are three gods or lords.

The Father was neither made nor created nor begotten from anyone.
The Son was neither made nor created;
he was begotten from the Father alone.
The Holy Spirit was neither made nor created nor begotten;
he proceeds from the Father and the Son.

Accordingly there is one Father, not three fathers;
there is one Son, not three sons;
there is one Holy Spirit, not three holy spirits.

Nothing in this trinity is before or after,
nothing is greater or smaller;
in their entirety the three persons
are coeternal and coequal with each other.

So in everything, as was said earlier,
we must worship their trinity in their unity
and their unity in their trinity.

Anyone then who desires to be saved
should think thus about the trinity.

But it is necessary for eternal salvation
that one also believe in the incarnation
of our Lord Jesus Christ faithfully.

Now this is the true faith:

That we believe and confess
that our Lord Jesus Christ, God's Son,
is both God and human, equally.

He is God from the essence of the Father,
begotten before time;
and he is human from the essence of his mother,
born in time;
completely God, completely human,
with a rational soul and human flesh;
equal to the Father as regards divinity,
less than the Father as regards humanity.

Although he is God and human,
yet Christ is not two, but one.
He is one, however,
not by his divinity being turned into flesh,
but by God's taking humanity to himself.
He is one,
certainly not by the blending of his essence,
but by the unity of his person.
For just as one human is both rational soul and flesh,
so too the one Christ is both God and human.

He suffered for our salvation;
he descended to hell;
he arose from the dead;
he ascended to heaven;
he is seated at the Father's right hand;
from there he will come to judge the living and the dead.
At his coming all people will arise bodily
and give an accounting of their own deeds.
Those who have done good will enter eternal life,
and those who have done evil will enter eternal fire.[1]

FURTHER STUDY

I want to extend my deep gratitude to the following preachers and teachers who have greatly contributed to my knowledge of the Trinity (and therefore to the content of this book):

- Tim Keller
- Fred Sanders
- Michael Reeves
- R. C. Sproul
- John Piper
- Wayne Grudem
- J. R. Vassar
- Bruce Ware
- Sam Allberry
- James R. White
- Donald Macleod

Other books on the Trinity

For a simple, straightforward overview:
- *Shared Life* by Donald Macleod

General overview:
- *The Deep Things of God: How the Trinity Changes Everything* by Fred Sanders

For historical context:
- *The Holy Trinity: In Scripture, History, Theology, and Worship* by Robert Letham

For an exploration of the original language:
- *The Forgotten Trinity: Recovering the Heart of Christian Belief* by James R. White

In relation to other world religions:
- *Delighting in the Trinity: An Introduction to the Christian Faith* by Michael Reeves

ENDNOTES

A Word from the Author

1. J. I. Packer, *Concise Theology* (Wheaton: Tyndale House Publishers, Inc., 1993), 40.

2. Augustine is sometimes credited with this.

3. "History of Trinitarian Doctrines," *Stanford Encyclopedia of Philosophy*, accessed April 21, 2021, https://plato.stanford.edu/entries/trinity/trinity-history.html.

4. Ligon Duncan, "How Is the Trinity Central to the Gospel?" TGC, October 4, 2017, accessed May 5, 2021, https://www.thegospelcoalition.org/video/trinity-central-gospel/.

Session Two

1. B. B. Warfield, as quoted by Justin Taylor in "B. B. Warfield 's Analogy for the Trinity in the Old Testament,"April 18, 2017, accessed April 26, 2021, https://www.thegospelcoalition.org/blogs/justin-taylor/b-b-warfields-analogy-for-the-trinity-in-the-old-testament//

2. Thomas Aquinas, *Theological Texts* (Oxford-University Press, 1955), 295.

3. Strong's H430, *Blue Letter Bible*, accessed April 26, 2021, https://www.blueletterbible.org/lang/lexicon/lexicon.cfm?t=kjv&strongs=h430.

4. Donald Macleod, *Shared Life* (UK: Christian Focus Publications, 2005), 13.

5. Wayne Grudem, *Systematic Theology* (Grand Rapids, MI: Zondervan, 1994), 255.

6. Matt Perman, "What Is the Doctrine of the Trinity," *desiringGod*, January 23, 2006, accessed April 21, 2021, https://www.desiringgod.org/articles/what-is-the-doctrine-of-the-trinity.

7. James R. White, *The Forgotten Trinity: Recovering the Heart of Christian Belief* (Ada, MI: Baker Books, 2019).

8. Fred Sanders, *The Deep Things of God* (Wheaton, IL: Crossway, 2017), 68.

9. Tim Keller, "The Triune God," June 12, 2011, accessed May 5, 2021, https://gospelinlife.com/downloads/the-triune-god-4908/.

10. *Oxford Dictionary*, s.v. "immanent," accessed April 26, 2021, https://www.lexico.com/en/definition/immanent.

11. Sanders, *The Deep Things of God*.

12. Ibid, 89.

13. Strong's G3621, *Blue Letter Bible*, accessed April 21, 2021, https://www.blueletterbible.org/lang/lexicon/lexicon.cfm?t=kjv&strongs=g362.

14. Sanders, *The Deep Things of God*.

15. Tim Keller, "The Glory of the Triune God," June 19, 2011, accessed May 5, 2021, https://gospelinlife.com/downloads/the-triune-god-4908/.

16. Sanders, 89.

Session Three

1. Michael Reeves, *Delighting in the Trinity* (Downers Grove, IL: IVP Academic, 2012), 111.

2. Sanders, *The Deep Things of God*.

3. J. I. Packer, *Knowing God* (Downers Grove, IL: IVP Books, 1973), 201.

4. Jonathan Edwards, *A Treatise Concerning Religious Affections* (Glasgow: W. Collins & Co., 1840) 77.

5. Reeves, *Delighting in the Trinity*.

6. "The Most Quoted Verse in the Bible," *Character of God*, Episode 1, *Bible Project Podcast*, August 17, 2020, https://bibleproject.com/podcast/most-quoted-verse-bible/.

7. "Overview of Food Ingredients, Additives & Color," *FDA*, November 2004, revised April 2010, https://www.fda.gov/food/food-ingredients-packaging/overview-food-ingredients-additives-colors#:~:text=Food%20manufacturers%20are%20required%20to,by%20those%20in%20smaller%20amounts.

Session Four

1. Bill Cook, *40 Days in Mark* (Nashville, TN: B&H Publishing, 2020).

2. Don Stewart, "What Does the Hebrew Term *Adonai* Stand For?," *Blue Letter Bible*, accessed April 12, 2021, https://www.blueletterbible.org/Comm/stewart_don/faq/the-attributes-of-god-that-belong-to-him-alone/21-what-does-the-hebrew-term-adonai-stand-for.cfm.

3. Strong's G3056, *Blue Letter Bible,* accessed April 12, 2021, https://www.blueletterbible.org/lang/lexicon/lexicon.cfm?Strongs=G3056&t=KJV.

4. Tim Chaffey, "Theophanies in the Old Testament," *Answers in Genesis*, January 13, 2012, accessed April 26, 2021, https://answersingenesis.org/jesus/incarnation/theophanies-in-the-old-testament/.

5. Strong's H43397, *Blue Letter Bible*, accessed April 12, 2021, https://www.blueletterbible.org/lang/lexicon/lexicon.cfm?Strongs=H4397&t=KJV.

6. John Owen, *The Person and Glory of Christ* (New York: Robert Carter & Brothers, 1852), 349–350.

7. Sanders, *The Deep Things of God*.

8. Richard R. Melick, Jr., *New American Commentary: Philippians, Colossians, Philemon*, Vol 32 (Nashville: B&H Publishing Group, 1991), 217.

9. Nicene Creed, accessed April 13, 2021, via https://www.marquette.edu/faith/prayers-nicene.php.

10. Ibid.

11. H. Richard Niebuhr, *The Kingdom of God in America* (Middleton, CN: Wesleyan University Press, 1968), 193.

12. David Mathis, "What Is the Hypostatic Union?," *desiringGod*, December 19, 2007, accessed April 12, 2021, https://www.desiringgod.org/articles/what-is-the-hypostatic-union.

13. Ulrik Nissen, *The Polity of Christ* (Great Britain: T&T Clark, Bloomsbury Publishing, 2020), 16.

14. R. C. Sproul, *The Work of Christ* (Colorado Springs: David C Cook, 2012), 8.

15. Martin Luther, *Luther's Works: Reformation writings and occasional pieces* (United States: Concordia, 1955), 316.

Session Five

1. Strong's H7307, *Blue Letter Bible,* accessed April 15, 2021, https://www.blueletterbible.org/lang/lexicon/lexicon.cfm?t=kjv&strongs=h7307.

2. Strong's G4151, *Blue Letter Bible,* accessed April 15, 2021, https://www.blueletterbible.org/lang/lexicon/lexicon.cfm?t=kjv&strongs=g4151.

3. James B. Torrance, *Worship, Community & the Triune Grace of God* (Downers Grove, IL: InterVarsity Press, 1996), 76.

4. Andy Naselli, "The Unpardonable Sin," *The Gospel Coalition,* accessed April 15, 2021, https://www.thegospelcoalition.org/essay/the-unpardonable-sin/.

Session Six

1. Tim Keller, Twitter, February 23, 2015, accessed April 19, 2021, https://twitter.com/timkellernyc/status/569890726349307904?lang=en.

2. Tim Chester, *Delighting in the Trinity* (UK: The Good Book Company, 2010).

3. C. S. Lewis, "Letter 21," *Letters to Malcolm: Chiefly on Prayer* (San Francisco: HarperOne, 2017, originally pub. 1963 by Harcourt Brace).

4. John Piper, as quoted by Jared Wilson in *Gospel Driven Ministry* (Grand Rapids, MI: Zondervan, 2021), 50.

5. Sanders, *The Deep Things of God,* 85.

6. Gerald Bray, as quoted by Sanders in *The Triune God* (Grand Rapids, MI: Zondervan, 2016).

7. Sam Allberry, "The Trinity and Christian Prayer," The Village church, interview, April 12, 2015, accessed April 26, 2021, https://5zu3o1glj423bhz11le70nbe-wpengine.netdna-ssl.com/wp-content/uploads/2020/04/201504121115FMWC21ASAAA_SamAllberry-TheTrinityandChristianPrayer.pdf.

8. Ibid.

9. Ibid.

10. James B. Torrance, *Worship, Community, & the Triune God of Grace* (Downers Grove, IL: InterVarsity Press, 1996), 15.

11. Emilie Griffin, *Clinging: The Experience of Prayer* (Wichita KS: Eighth Day Press, 2003), 7–8.

12. John Piper, When I Don't Desire God (Wheaton, IL: Crossway, 2004), 167.

13. Tim Keller, Twitter, November 10, 2014, accessed April 20, 2021, https://twitter.com/timkellernyc/status/531906966550228993?lang=en.

Session Seven

1. Richard Sibbes, as quoted by Sanders in *The Deep Things of God.*

2. Macleod, *Shared Life,* 58–59.

3. Macleod, *Shared Life,* 87.

4. Macleod, *Shared Life,* 85.

5. Reeves, *Delighting in the Trinity,* 10.

6. Reeves, *The Good God* (Crownhill, Milton Keynes: Paternoster, 2012).

7. Blaise Pascal, *The Harvard Classics* (U.S.A.: P. F. Collier & Son, 1910), 138.

8. Tim Keller, *The Reason for God* (New York: Penguin Books, 2018), 229.

9. Macleod, *Shared Life,* 79.

10. Strong's G3101, *Blue Letter Bible,* accessed April 23, 2021, https://www.blueletterbible.org/lang/lexicon/lexicon.cfm?t=esv&strongs=g3101.

Glossary

1. *Merriam-Webster,* s.v. "consubstantial," accessed April 26, 2021, https://www.merriam-webster.com/dictionary/consubstantial.

2. Don Stewart, "What Is Christian Teaching?," *Blue Letter Bible,* accessed April 26, 2021, https://www.blueletterbible.org/Comm/stewart_don/faq/bible-basics/question2-what-is-christian-doctrine.cfm.

3. "What Is the Economic and Immanent Trinity?," *Zondervan Academic,* April 27, 2018, accessed April 26, 2021, https://zondervanacademic.com/blog/what-is-the-economic-and-immanent-trinity.

4. *Merriam-Webster,* s.v. "glorify," accessed April 26, 2021. https://www.merriam-webster.com/dictionary/glorify.

5. David Mathis, "What Is the Hypostatic Union?," *desiringGod,* December 19, 2007, accessed April 26, 2021, https://www.desiringgod.org/articles/what-is-the-hypostatic-union.

6. What Is the Economic and Immanent Trinity?," *Zondervan Academic.*

7. Don Stewart, "What Is a Monotheistic Religion?," *Blue Letter Bible*, accessed April 26, 2021, https://www.blueletterbible.org/faq/don_stewart/don_stewart_299.cfm.

8. Don Stewart, "What Is Polytheism?," *Blue Letter Bible*, accessed April 26, 2021, https://www.blueletterbible.org/faq/don_stewart/don_stewart_303.cfm.

9. Don Stewart, "What Is Progressive Revelation?," accessed April 26, 2021, https://www.blueletterbible.org/faq/don_stewart/don_stewart_1203.cfm.

10. Don Stewart, "What Is Christian Theology?," accessed April 26, 2021, https://www.blueletterbible.org/Comm/stewart_don/faq/bible-basics/question1-what-is-christian-theology.cfm.

11. BibleStudyTools, s.v. "Theophany," accessed April 26, 2021, https://www.biblestudytools.com/dictionary/theophany/.

Heresies

1. *Merriam-Webster*, s.v. "Arianism," accessed April 26, 2021, https://www.merriam-webster.com/dictionary/arianism.

2. *Merriam-Webster*, s.v. "Docetism," accessed April 26, 2021, https://www.merriam-webster.com/dictionary/Docetism.

3. *Merriam-Webster*, s.v. "gnosticism," accessed April 26, 2021, https://www.merriam-webster.com/dictionary/gnosticism.

4. *Merriam-Webster*, s.v. "henotheism," accessed April 26, 2021, https://www.merriam-webster.com/dictionary/henotheism

5. *Merriam-Webster*, s.v. "modalism," accessed April 26, 2021, https://www.merriam-webster.com/dictionary/modalism.

6. *Merriam-Webster*, s.v. "monarchianism," accessed April 26, 2021, https://www.merriam-webster.com/dictionary/monarchianism.

7. *Merriam-Webster*, s.v. "monophysitism," accessed April 26, 2021, https://www.merriam-webster.com/dictionary/monophysitism.

8. *Merriam-Webster*, s.v. "nestorianism," accessed April 26, 2021, https://www.merriam-webster.com/dictionary/nestorianism.

9. *Merriam-Webster*, s.v. "polytheism," accessed April 26, 2021, https://www.merriam-webster.com/dictionary/polytheism.

10. *Merriam-Webster*, s.v. "subordinationism," accessed April 26, 2021, https://www.merriam-webster.com/dictionary/subordinationism.

11. *Merriam-Webster*, s.v. "tritheism," accessed April 26, 2021, https://www.merriam-webster.com/dictionary/tritheism.

12. *Merriam-Webster*, s.v. "unitarianism," accessed April 26, 2021, https://www.merriam-webster.com/dictionary/unitarianism.

Athanasian Creed

1. "Athanasian Creed," *CRCNA*, accessed April 23, 2021, https://www.crcna.org/welcome/beliefs/creeds/athanasian-creed.

In this adaptation for teenagers, Tara-Leigh takes students on the same journey to carefully and biblically pull back the curtain and get a clear view of the Trinity. Students will examine each of the Persons of God—Father, Son, and Spirit—and discover that joy comes from delighting in who He is.
Learn more and find a sample:
lifeway.com/wherethejoyis
7-SESSION BIBLE STUDY FOR TEENS
HE'S WHERE THE JOY IS
GETTING TO KNOW THE CAPTIVATING GOD OF THE TRINITY
TARA-LEIGH COBBLE
Study
together.
Lifeway students

Get the most from your study.

Customize your Bible study time with a guided experience.

Join Tara-Leigh Cobble in this 7-session study as she breaks down the intimidating doctrine of the Trinity. You'll discover a beautiful, foundational view of our triune God that will transform how you relate to Him. Understanding God's three-in-oneness and each of the Persons of God individually—Father, Son, and Spirit—will lead you to deeper intimacy with God and greater joy in knowing Him!

In this study you'll:

- Learn about the unity and diversity of the Trinity.

- Explore the roles of each person of the Trinity.

- Unpack theological truths about prayer and how we can commune with and talk to God.

- Understand how to apply the truth of who God is in the Trinity to your everyday life and how you can relate to Him.

To enrich your study experience, consider the accompanying *He's Where the Joy Is* video or audio teaching sessions. Although you can complete the study without the video or audio sessions, each session packs fundamental truths into approximately 15–20 minutes of teaching from Tara-Leigh Cobble.

Studying on your own or with a friend? Watch or listen to Tara-Leigh Cobble's teaching sessions, available for rent or purchase at lifeway.com/wherethejoyis.

Leading a group? Our leader kits are designed for leaders and make it easy to get your group started. (Leader kit includes one *He's Where the Joy Is* Bible study book, DVDs with teaching videos, and teaching video downloads for three additional users.) Get yours at lifeway.com/wherethejoyis.

ADDITIONAL RESOURCES

Visit **lifeway.com/ wherethejoyis** to explore the entire study family— *Bible study book, leader kit, Bible study eBook, video teaching sessions,* and *audio teaching sessions—* along with a free session sample, video clips, and church promotional materials.